K.

The Diamond Fields of South Africa

With Notes of Journey there and homeward

K.

The Diamond Fields of South Africa
With Notes of Journey there and homeward

ISBN/EAN: 9783743454729

Printed in Europe, USA, Canada, Australia, Japan

Cover: Foto ©Suzi / pixelio.de

More available books at **www.hansebooks.com**

THE

DIAMOND FIELDS

OF

SOUTH AFRICA;

WITH

NOTES OF JOURNEY THERE AND HOMEWARD,

AND

SOME THINGS ABOUT DIAMONDS AND OTHER JEWELS.

———

BY

ONE WHO HAS VISITED THE FIELDS.

———

NEW YORK:
AMERICAN NEWS COMPANY,
119 NASSAU STREET.
1872.

CONTENTS.

PREFACE.

It has been the object of the author in this little work to present a true account of the Diamond Fields near the Vaal River, in Southern Africa, together with a statement of the various routes and modes of travel to the mines, including brief sketches of objects of interest met with on his journey going and returning.

When it was determined to write a few pages on the above subject, which was begun while in Africa, it was thought that there was more interest in America concerning the Vaal Fields than perhaps there really is, and that any information in reference to them would be very acceptable. It was reported at the " Diggings " in March last that several vessels had arrived from the United States at the Cape of Good Hope with many passengers for the mines; at one time it was said three hundred had landed at Port Elizabeth; at another, one hundred and fifty at Natal; and still at another, over one hundred at Cape Town. But those reports must have been untrue or greatly exaggerated, as the author met with no such number at any place; yet there are many Americans on the Fields, and more were going to them from the different ports in March and April.

Notwithstanding, the work has been submitted to the public, hoping it may prove interesting to the general reader—especially with the addition of a few pages about precious stones, which

2

have been compiled from various authorities and presented in
a concise form, showing when and where they have been principally found in the different ages of the world; their antiquity,
properties, and characteristics, taken from the standard authorities on the subject. It is, perhaps, needless to say that the
author has no interest to promote in this publication, except
the interest all writers must feel in the success of their labors.
He has been to the South African Diamond Fields from the
United States and returned again to the same country, compos-
ing his "notes of travel" chiefly on the homeward voyage at
sea, and all is now submitted to the hands of the reader.

K.

THE

DIAMOND FIELDS

OF

SOUTH AFRICA.

CHAPTER I.

TO ENGLAND.

In August, 1870, the first accounts of the discovery
of diamonds on the banks of the Vaal River, in South
Africa, were published in the United States. At that
time, desiring to take a voyage upon the sea, to learn
more of the world, and to obtain some knowledge of
foreign countries by experience and observation, I re-
solved, as soon as circumstances would permit, to direct
my course toward the newly-discovered "Golconda,"
as it was then called; therefore, on Saturday, the 17th
day of December, 1870, having obtained a passage to
Liverpool, England, by the good ship "Nestorian," of
the Allan Line of mail steamers, I went on board that
ship, which was then lying in the harbor of Portland,
Maine, and at eight o'clock in the evening of the same day
she steamed beautifully and grandly out of the port, salu-
ting, as she passed, the American flag and forts over
which it waved, by the discharge of two cannon, and

soon we were far out on the broad Atlantic, driven rapidly on our course by the favoring winds and rolling
sea. The voyage across the ocean was pleasant for the
season of winter, and quickly performed. Early on the
morning of the 27th of December the rocky coast of the
North of Ireland became visible ; during the day, which
was calm and bright, the vessel passed along the coast
very near the rocks on which the Cambria struck but a
short time before, and with all on board save one was
buried beneath the relentless waves. At about noon,
the mails for Londonderry were discharged at the mouth
of the River Foyle ; then, steaming among the rocky
isles, past the Giant's Causeway, round the coast of the
Emerald Land, the scenery was sometimes beautiful
and picturesque, romantic, and at others, bleak, barren
and desolate ; while, entering Lough Foyle, the shore
was thickly dotted with snug little cottages, and far up
the gently sloping coast could be seen the narrow fields
and thatched homes of the irrepressible man. At one
place, a romantic little scene of a cottage, with lawn
down to the shore and walks shaded with evergreen
trees, with a fountain bubbling up in the midst, was
pointed out as belonging to one who had become an
American, and having acquired a large fortune in his
adopted country, had purchased and adorned his place
of birth. At another point the ruins of Green Castle
were seen, being the remains of the walls and turrets of
an old stone building covered with green ivy, around
whose antiquity, as around all the works of long-buried
hands, the human mind casts so much vain and useless
veneration. Then, passing the Giant's Causeway,

where is presented one of the most dreary and desolate-looking places which can be imagined—high, perpendicular rocks jutting here and there out from the main land, forming vast caverns for a number of miles along the coast, enveloped in a smoky, dismal atmosphere; one more night upon the sea, and on the 28th day of December the steamer entered the Mersey, and we were soon permitted to go ashore over the landing stage at Liverpool.

The feelings of every individual while on their first voyage upon the boundless ocean are doubtless mingled with awe and wonder. There is not a pen that has yet been able to fully paint or describe the beauty and calmness of the "quiet sea," or the power, grandeur and sublimity of the rolling waves when the tempest lifts them up. That the low and uneven coast should confine its billows within their proper bounds and fix a sure line, saying, as it were, in the voice of command, "Hitherto shalt thou come, but no further: and here shall thy proud waves be staid," but leads us to conclude that some Omnipotent Being "holds the sea as in the hollow of His hand," and that His power can move the great waves or still the tempest.

The passage of the Nestorian from Portland to Liverpool was accomplished in little less than eleven days. After taking the needful rest and refreshment, I proceeded to a rapid survey of the reputed greatest commercial city of the world.

Liverpool is situated on the northern bank of the River Mersey, in the northwest of England. It contains upwards of five hundred thousand inhabitants, and is noted for its ten miles of docks for shipping, and the vast labor of their construction. At this port much of the trade and commerce of Britain is carried on; here the immense quantity of cotton and wool manufactured by the numberless looms of Manchester and other towns is received, and in the shape of fabrics again sent out to be distributed over the whole world.

A place of its wealth, of course, has many fine buildings and monuments, not the least of which is the Exchange, but recently completed, and the railway stations are built on a scale of capacity and durability fully commensurate to the requirements of the city.

On the 29th day of December, leaving Liverpool by taking the cars at the Lime-street Station at one o'clock P.M., I arrived in London at the Euston Station at seven o'clock, performing the distance of two hundred and one miles in six hours.

The cars in England are constructed quite differently from those in America; but I saw none that could compare with the Pulman palace drawing-room cars of my own country, either in beauty and richness, or convenience and comfort. The cars are shorter than the American, and the first and second class have several compartments in each car. In the third class there are no divisions; the seats face each other and extend wholly across the car, and they are entered by doors on either side. I believe no stoves or fires are allowed, but the feet can be kept warm with a tin heater filled with hot water. The entrance at the sides is, doubtless, as to accidents, an improvement on the American method of entering at the end; and it prevents the

crowding and rush usual in filling a car at the two end
doors; and also passengers can get their seats much
quicker, for in the English only two seats can be filled
from one entrance, and much less time is required;
aside from that, I prefer the style of the American cars.

After arriving in London the first consideration was
"business before pleasure," and acting on that maxim
I soon procured a passage by steamship to South Af.
rica.

It may be proper here to state that when my journey
was commenced, there was not, nor is there now, any
line of steamers, nor in fact any steamships, running
from the United States to South Africa, and when I
started I could not learn there were any sailing vessels on board which one could obtain a passage to that
country. But now I am informed there is a regular
line of sailing vessels from Boston to the Cape of Good
Hope, leaving Boston once a month; besides, there are
other ships occasionally sailing from Boston or New
York, on board which, doubtless, a passage can be procured should any one be persuaded, by the glowing accounts he may read of the rich soil and growing pros-
pects of Cape Colony and the Diamond Fields, to
journey that way. But if any one desires to journey
there by steamships, the only route is by way of England, and to that country it is not necessary to make
any mention of the various lines of steamers, nor of
the rates of passage, as they are numerous, and fully
published by circulars and advertisements.

From England to Cape Town, Algoa Bay, and Port
Natal, on the Southern coast of Africa, there is a regu·

lar line of the Union Mail Steamship Company's steamers that leave Southampton, England, twice every month—the 8th and 21st, for these places, with very good passenger accommodations. There is also another line, called, I think, the Cape of Good Hope Steamship Company, but the charges are the same, or very nearly, (to Cape Town from London, £21 second-class ; £31 first-class ; to Algoa Bay, £23 2s. second-class ; £34 first-class.

Having secured my passage to Port Elizabeth, Algoa Bay, by the Union Mail Steamship Company's steamer, "Celt," which was to sail from Southampton on the 8th day of January, 1871, I had about one week to spend in the great city of London, where almost unconsciously I found myself roaming about. There is in this city an underground railway, built in nearly a circle round it. In my first walk wishing to proceed from Euston station to Moorgate street, a distance of about three miles, I took the cars on this road at Gower street. Trains of from five to ten cars pass each way every five minutes. At the entrance to a station on the ground-floor a ticket is procured at the office, which is passed on the way, for any station it may be desired to get off, the fare being so much per mile ; then passing down a staircase arched with glass set in iron, at the foot of the steps the ticket is checked by a clerk there, when stepping out on the platform the passenger awaits the arrival of the train. The platforms are lighted sometimes by sky-light and sometimes with gas ; they are wide, extending up and down some distance, and everything shows neatness and order in the management of the road. The cars come up rapidly, stop quite quickly; the platform being level with the floor of the car and quite up to it, one steps in at the side door, the guard cries *right*, and with a sharp whistle the train moves quickly along. The stoppage at each station is but very little longer than that required of a horse car for the entrance of one passenger. Each compartment of the car is lighted; being seated, one glides smoothly over the well built road, and if familiar with the streets and stations at which it is desired to stop, can read the morning papers with but very little jostling; arriving at his destination and leaving the cars, the passenger ascends another stair-case where his ticket is taken, and he passes out upon the street to which he wished to go. I rode to and fro on these cars a number of times; from what I saw and could learn of the road, it must be a very successful institution.

On Sunday morning of January 1, I attended the services of the English church held in Westminster Abbey. Doubtless the reader will surmise the truth, that curiosity led me on this bright and beautiful Sabbath, and on new year's morning, to that old and, to the English, venerable structure that has stood the storms of so many centuries, and round whose ancient pillars there clusters at once so many of England's illustrious dead and the history of their lives. To enter upon a minute description or history of the Abbey and its various cloisters and chapels, would be giving it too great prominence and extending this book far beyond the limits which are at present decided upon, besides requiring material and research not at present at the

2*

author's command. Every visitor can provide himself
at the Abbey doors, as he enters, with a small work
giving all needful information.

The sermon this New Year's morning was delivered
by the Rev. John Jennings, Archdeacon of Westminster; the services were performed by a number of as-
sistants. The Abbey contains a large organ, and a full
choir were in attendance who sung the responses from
behind a screen in one of the cloisters. After the services were concluded the audience were permitted to
enter the chapels and view the monuments and tombs
containing the remains and erected in honor of the
memories of many of England's greatest men, both
those who had sat on her throne or in her legislative
chambers or halls of justice, as well as those who had
led her armies to battle upon land or sea, or had raised
themselves from humble positions in life to be ornaments to their race and the times in which they lived.

The use for which the building was originally constructed has been entirely perverted; it is now used
principally as a receptacle for the mortal remains of the
great and good of the kingdom.

The latest burial at this time was that of Charles
Dickens, whose tomb was under the pavement of the
Southern transept to the main building, and on which
fresh flowers woven into a coronet were laid "Lord,
ever keep my memory green." Dickens, the humble
architect of his own fame and fortune, sleeps his last
sleep under the same roof with the most noble, most
powerful, and most proud and haughty of seven centuries of England's greatness, and although he had no

ambition for such a place of rest, yet kings and princes
love to be buried by the side of such humble worth, for
Dickens will be read and remembered for his kindness
of heart and encouraging "words" by thousands of
grateful beings, long after the memory of the proud kings
and princes who sleep beside him has sunk into irre-
trievable oblivion.

Here in Westminster I also found a mournful monument to the cruel fates of war. Ah! indeed, to what
fate will you not find a monument here erected? It
cannot be of rulers, for many of them are there; it cannot be of warriors, for many of them lie beneath tombs
covered with their steel armor; it cannot be of legisla-
tors, or counsellors, or ministers, for there their bodies
rest, one above the other, crowding each other even
more than when life flowed through their veins; it cannot be jutisces, judges or chancellors, for there rests
the great Mansfield, with many other great luminaries
of the Bench and Bar. But here at last rests the body
of the unfortunate Major André, cut down in the full
career of early manhood, and when royal favors had
raised him at an early period of life to a high position
in the British army. I believe every true American, if
not as an Englishman, will yet feel sad at the fate of
this accomplished young man as well as at the circumstances which led to his untimely death, and the treach-
ery of an American whose death should have been his.
A fine monument to his memory stands on the right
side from the front entrance, consisting of solid marble,
surmounted by a beautiful statue of a lady with a melancholy expression, bending over with looks cast down ;

and on a moulded panelled base and plinth stands a sarcophagus, on the panel of which is inscribed "Sacred to the memory of Major John André, who, raised by his merits at an early period of life to the rank of Adjutant General of the British forces in America, and employed in an important but hazardous enterprise, fell a sacrifice to his zeal for his king and country on the 2d of October, 1780, aged 29. Universally beloved and esteemed by the army in which he served, and lamented even by his foes, his gracious sovereign, King George III., has caused this "monument to be erected," and on the plinth, "the remains of the said Major André were deposited on the 28th November, 1821, in a grave near this monument." But no marble slab in honor of the memory of the man whose actions resulted in the death of this noble youth speaks of a grateful sovereign or people, and his grave doubtless lies in the obscurity that should cover his name.

In this cathedral also the solemn offices of crowning and enthroning the sovereigns of England takes place ; here they assume that authority which they lay off but to have their bodies carried back and placed beneath the roof from which they departed with regal dignities. In the centre of the sacrarium, and beneath the lantern, is erected the throne at which the peers do homage. When the crowns are put on, the peers and peeresses put on their coronets, and a signal is given from the top of the Abbey for the tower guns to fire at the same instant. To take an advantageous view of the inside of the Abbey, one must stand at the west door between the two towers, when the whole body of the church opens itself at once before the eye, which cannot but fill the mind of every beholder with the awful solemnity of the place. The loftiness of the roof, over one hundred feet from the pavement, the happy disposition of the lights, and the noble range of pillars by which the whole building is supported, all tend their influence to remind one that it is but a lonely place, and fit tomb for buried greatness.

On leaving the Abbey, at about two o'clock in the afternoon, people were seen streaming from all directions towards some particular point. Making inquiry as to the place of attraction, I learned it was the ice in St. James's Park; and it not being far away I fell into the current, and was soon in the Park, witnessing the sliding and skating of the people on the ice. It must have been the poorer class who were seeking amusement in this way on a Sunday afternoon—the people who during the week find no leisure moments to spend in recreation and exercise, and on Sunday their natures break forth from the calm and quiet of a Sabbath in the country; and on this day they assembled here to spend their few hours of freedom in social life and activity. But the attraction of the ice could not have been great, for it was quite rough and covered with snow, except where here and there a small spot had been swept. A New Yorker, with his magnificent skating park, would hardly attempt to find amusement on such ice as was found in St. James's Park at this time; yet here were assembled countless thousands—a fair representation of the vast crowds that, in this metropolis of the world, will ever flock to any point of attraction, be it the triumphal pro-

cession of order and law, or the tumultuous gathering
of riot and confusion for the purposes of crime and destruction.   Leaving the Park, and passing under the
Horse Guards (or war office), the buildings from
which all military operations are conducted, by White-
hall, Nelson's Monument, etc., I took my way to my
lodgings.   In the evening of the same Sabbath, the
next place of greatest interest and attraction to the
stranger that occurred to my mind, was St. Paul's
Cathedral.

England boasts that the sun never sets on her dominions, and that the prayers of her church ascend to
heaven every hour of the twenty-four, and unceasingly
throughout the rolling years, in some part of her realms,
the anthems of praise are constantly being sung.   And
St. Paul's is the grand centre over all her wide ecclesi-
astical domain.   Notices were published that the services of the English Church would be held there at the
usual hour in the evening, and that the sermon would
be delivered by the Bishop of London.   Accordingly,
seven o'clock found me ascending the steps of this
church.   Entering the building at the main vestibule,
one is unexpectedly filled with surprise and wonder at
the grandeur of the columns, the loftiness of the ceiling,
and the strength, solidity and massiveness of the whole.
Here, too, every one must have a feeling of solemnity
when for the first time entering such a cathedral, whose
massive walls, pillars and vestibules have for nearly
two hundred years echoed to the footsteps, to the
prayers and praises, to the choral songs and anthems,
to the eloquent and solemn voice of warning, reverber-

ated by many generations, not only of the masses of high and low of London, but doubtless of the stranger from all parts of the world.

Passing along to the sitting space, I took my seat under the dome in front of the organ and choir—the great space arched by the dome, and far out in the vestibules, extending either way. The coming throngs soon filled the place.

The organ intoned its warning notes, while some two or three hundred singers—mostly men and boys—all in white surplices, took their seats in the choir before the organ. The clergymen took their several stations, and the services commenced in all the pomp of the Church of England, the choir singing the responses throughout the whole.

The sermon was delivered by the Bishop. It would be hardly possible for any man to stand up in such a place, before such an audience, to speak upon the great principles of life and the attractions of a future world, without experiencing a thrill of eloquence stirring him to action ; and the attentive listener will depart with, to say the least, a sober and thoughtful mind ; and as you leave the sacred walls of the temple of God, a small tract is presented, with a view, no doubt, of impressing the lessons just taught more firmly upon the thoughts of the hearer.

In the erection of St. Paul's, London intended to rival the world in any similar construction, both in its size and magnificence, and at the time the cathedral was completed she probably may have succeeded in the enterprise.

The first stone of the present (called new) building was laid June 21st, 1675, by the architect Sir Christopher Wren. Twenty-two years elapsed from the laying of the first stone to the opening of the choir for divine service.

On the 2d day of December, 1697, the services of dedication were performed. In the year 1710, the exterior was adjudged to be complete, and it stood with its perfect dome and encircling colonnades, its galleries, and ball, and surmounting cross ; and in that year Sir Christopher, by the hand of his son, attended by Mr. Strong, the master mason who had superintended the whole work, laid the last and highest stone of the lantern of the cupola. Whether Sir Christopher stood on the ground beneath or on the giddy height, to witness this final act to his great work, does not seem to be known. At least, it must have been a scene of supreme pleasure and limitless joy to him, with the crowding thousands standing round to witness the final completion of such a work, all the creation of his own mind ; the whole building stretching out in all its perfect harmony, with its line horizontal lines, various, yet in perfect unison, its towers, its unrivalled dome, its crowning lantern and cross—all so beautiful and great in its symmetry and perfection.

On Monday, January 2d, and the following days, the places of note I visited were : first, the House of Parliament, where the stranger is politely shown around by a lady in attendance, who has an appointment for that purpose, and the uniformed and liveried men standing in the passages and halls are not allowed to interfere

with her perquisites. The seats of Mr. Gladstone, and
of Disraeli, his opponent; of the Marquis of Lorne,
since married to the Princess Louise; and of other no
tables in the House of Commons; the ladies' gallery,
back of and above the chair; the Bar of the House,
where members are placed for any violation of order;
and the manner of the proceedings were all kindly explained by my fair conductress.

I next visited Victoria Tower, where the crown
jewels are kept, the chief attraction which led me there
being the famous diamond Kohinoor. Being about to
enter upon the business of picking up diamonds, of
course my curiosity was awakened to see a gem whose
fame and lustre might be obscured by something I
should find. After saying so much, perhaps, lest the
reader's hopes in the future should be disappointed, it
might be well here to state, for the safety of the renown
and value of that unrivalled stone, that I found nothing
in the diamond fields of South Africa, during the short
time I remained there, to successfully compete with
the Kohinoor. It possibly may have been because I did
not labor long enough. There is but little doubt, according to many of the publications in Cape Colony,
but that if a person works a sufficient period of time
and spends a good large sum of money, he will find
gems to far exceed in size, value, and brilliancy, this
great diamond; or if he should be so unfortunate as not
to "pick up" one so great, he will at least find an
awful pile of little ones. But I am straying. After
obtaining permission from the proper officer, the crown
jewels are shown by a person in custody of them.

Another place of great interest to the visitor in London is the British Museum. Here one can spend a day or many days, as time and taste permits or inclines, with both pleasure and profit to the student of nature or art. It would be useless in a few lines to attempt to speak of its many and varied departments, and the fullness and completeness of each. It must be a great point of attraction to Londoners as well as to strangers. The collections are originals, and from all parts of the world. From every land and sea, from every clime, one will here find some memento to speak of its forests, its plains, its rocks or mountains, its thriving industry or ruined cities, its oceans and rivers ; all and every species of the known world will doubtless here find a representative.

I also visited the Bank of England and other places, such as the Royal Exchange, theatres, General Post Office, and other government buildings, where the dignitaries of the kingdom now, or in past ages, have held their regal sway.

I was obliged to go to the Bank of England to have its notes exchanged for coin, as the notes do not circulate in the Colonies, while British "sovereigns," a gold coin of the value of one pound sterling, I believe is at par in them all. The notes must be endorsed with the name and address of the bearer, when, if found to be genuine, a corner is torn off, intimating payment, and their value counted and weighed out to the presentor in gold or silver coin, as desired.

CHAPTER II.

HAVING procured my ticket for a passage to South Africa of the agents in London, Falconer & Mercer, at No. 3 East India Chambers, Leadenhall street, I was provided with a railroad pass free to Southampton, the place of sailing; therefore, on Sunday, the 8th day of January, leaving the great metropolis and all its busy, thronging people, with its deep misery and poverty, and its great wealth and profusion all commingled in one vast whirling maelstrom of existence, I was soon on board the steamer "Celt," bound for Cape Town and Algoa Bay. Although I had left my friends on the other side of the broad Atlantic, yet the scenes of parting, at the docks of Southampton, of the passengers from their relatives and friends, were as affecting to witness as such parting moments in life's pilgrimage ever are.

Here the widowed mother was for the first time separating from her son, who was leaving his native shores to tempt the dangers of the great deep, and to experience the realities of the untried, selfish world; filial love and parental care and tenderness were now to be parted, the mother to seek her lonely home and there await the rolling years for the day when declining age shall have fully wrought its work, and the last sands of life shall mark the hour of the setting

spirit; the son to be borne away with the buoyant
wings of youth, and the strength and vigor of early
manhood to a land seven thousand miles away, in whose
clime he expects to seek fame and fortune, and with all
his high hopes and ambition, he reflects that he may
find a watery grave far out on the restless ocean, or ere
his wishes are accomplished, the unsuitable winds of
another clime may lay him low in a foreign land, and
the mother and son commingle their tears, which flow
as in childhood's early years.

Again, there the father presses the hand of his
emancipated child, and gives him the hearty, "God
bless you, my boy, may you meet with success and soon
safely return." Friends press round departing friends,
all eyes express anxiety and care and love. The signal is given, the last word must be spoken, and the
decks of our moving home must be taken; the bridges
are drawn away, the ship moves slowly from the shore,
the last look is given, the last signal wave is made, the
vessel's speed increases, and on this clear, cold, yet
bright and beautiful Sabbath evening, pressing swiftly
out to sea, we soon are far from the sight of land, home,
or friends; and looking whithersoever we may, nought
but the ever moving waters will answer back our gaze.
On the first day out all seemed to be more or less de-
pressed with a sad and lonely spirit, and each one sought
to commune with his own thoughts and feelings rather
than the society of others; consequently, as the land re-
ceded from view, the passengers retired to their several
cabins, the officers gave their commands, and quiet and
order were soon established on the decks of the ship.

Subsequently I ascertained that there were sixty-five or sixty-six passengers aboard. The distance of the voyage from England to South Africa is about seven thousand miles. The time allowed this line of mail steamers to perform it, is, I am informed, thirty-eight days. But they seldom take the full time, the passage being usually accomplished in from thirty to thirty-three days. The "Celt" arrived in Cape Town the thirty-third day out from England. The following day, after leaving Southampton, the steamer touched at Plymouth, to take on the mails, and then sailed from Old England's shores with her prow turned direct towards the Island of Maderia, which lies a distance of about twelve hundred miles on the way. During the first few days, the weather was very stormy and the raging of the sea was fearful and wonderful to behold. The Bay of Biscay is noted for its terribly rough and resistless storms, especially in the season of winter, and at the time we were crossing it in January, old Neptune seemed to be lashing the waves with all the fury of "offended wrath." And here I witnessed all the grandeur of "a storm at sea," in the fullest sense of that phrase. Our great ship was tossed by the mounting waves as though its burden were but an atom ; every billow with great violence rolled over her decks. During the tempest three of the life boats which were swung lashed to their places a number of feet above the deck, were swept away with other gearing, and three of the seamen, while attempting to save the boats, were being carried away by the dashing waves, when they were rescued by the intervening "ratlins" to the

rigging, to which they clung till the sea had passed over.

No one can fully understand the power, grandeur, and sublimity of the ocean, except by seeing it when lashed into fury by the tempest, no more than the loneliness and awful solitude that is felt when in the midst of the calm, smooth sea can be understood unless it be individually experienced.

"No mortal measure swells that mystic sound,
No mortal minstrel breathes such tones around."

After six days of exceedingly rough weather, during which many had suffered all the horrors of sea-sickness, the Island of Maderia gladdened our sight on the morning of the 16th of January, and its lofty mountains, whose sides were covered with green verdure and growing grain and fruits, and dotted here and there with white cottages, was a great relief to the monotony we had experienced; not only because it was the solid earth on which our sea-sick bodies and tottering steps might again assume the semblance of firmness and youth; but also because we had only six days before left the cold, bleak shores of England, whose hills and valleys were covered with snow, and whose chilling winds had compelled one to wrap his heavy cloak about him, and to tie down the mufflers about his head and neck and stamp his freezing feet, while here the green hills and growing crops, brightened with the warm rays of the sun, would lead one to believe that the summer season, as well as the sight of land, had all at once broke upon us. The ship came to anchor off Funchal, the chief town of the Island,

situate on the southeast coast, at one o'clock P. M.
The harbor master came out in a small boat, and procured the bill of health of the passengers, after which
we were permitted to go ashore. Madeira is situate off
the northwestern coast of Africa, and 380 miles from
it, in latitude 32 dg. north, longitude 16 dg. west, and
belongs to or is under the government of Portugal,
and has remained a dependency of that country since
its discovery in the fifteenth century.

The productions of this island are various; in consequence of the altitude of its mountains almost every
degree of temperature is obtained. Nearly every European vegetable is cultivated with advantage, and
many of the productions of the tropics are obtained in
abundance, such as guavas, citrons, oranges, bananas
coffees, etc. But it is principally famed for the excellence of its climate, which is considered to be the finest
in the world, and is much resorted to by consumptive
patients.

The Island may be described as a mass of basalt
rising with a rather steep ascent from the south and
north towards the interior, where the mountains are of
considerable elevation, and interrupted by many deep
and narrow valleys, which are frequently traversed by
streams of excellent water, and in these valleys the
vineyards and gardens are chiefly situated, some of
them at an elevation of 2,000 feet above the level of
the sea. As the land is approached you discover the
green patches which are everywhere scattered over the
the deep red soil, even to the tops of the highest peaks.
This mountain verdure is owing to groves of heath

and broom, which grows to an extraordinary height; in
addition to these groves, on a closer approach, the
terraced acclivities, covered with a luxuriant tropical
vegetation, changes its distant barren aspect into one of
extreme beauty and fertility.

Some of the mountains are of considerable height;
the most lofty is that of Ruivo, which is 6,056 feet above
the sea. One of the greatest curiosities of Madeira is
the Curral, and to lovers of natural scenery it is well
worth the trouble of a visit. It is an immense valley
of almost fathomless depth, enclosed on all sides by a
range of magnificent mountain precipices 1,000 feet
high. Round a part of these cliffs is a narrow road cut
out of the rock, leading to the garden houses and country plantations. Riding along this road, the Curral
seems like a deep abyss, filled only with clouds and vapors, rolling in a constant motion over each other.
Sometimes the cliffs are black and craggy; at others,
they are covered with turf of the richest green and
trees indigenous to the island; while far below, smiles
a region of cultivation and fruitfulness, the white cabins
of the inhabitants, scattered over the surface of the
country, almost hidden amongst the rich gardens and
orchards.

In 1838, Commodore Wilkes, of the United States
Navy, visited this place, and in describing it he says :
" This is a very remarkable spot, and it is difficult, if not
impossible, to give an idea of its beauty and grandeur. It
is approached by the usual ascent from Funchal, through
the narrow roads or paths hedged with roses, etc., the
view gradually extending beneath, over the terraced

vineyards. Just before reaching it, you mount a small
ascent; you are then on the summit or edge of the Curral, and the whole scene suddenly bursts upon you.
The eye descends to the depth of 2,000 feet into the
immense chasm below, and wanders over the rugged
and broken outline of the many peaks that rise from its
very bottom; then upwards, following the grey precipitous rocks, till their summits are lost in the clouds,
which are passing fitfully across it, occasionally per-
mitting the sunbeams to glance to its very bottom.
One feels surprised, on gazing on this scene, that its
character of wildness should become softened, and its
beauty increased, which is effected in part by the plants
and shrubs, which cling or have fastened themselves
into the fissures of the rocks. These the eye gradually
makes out, and is led by the small and narrow strips of
green on the ledges downwards, until it finally rests on
the secluded church of Nostra Senora de Livre Monte,
and the peasants' cabin, imbedded in the dark and luxuriant foliage beneath, whose peace and quietness are in
such strong contrast with the wildness of nature above.
The whole looks more like enchantment than reality.
* * * * In the descent the road winds along the
sides of the precipice, turning around sharp and jutting
projections, with a frightful gulf yawning below. A
misstep of the horse would plunge the rider to destruction. At every turn new and striking views are
brought out, almost surpassing in grandeur the first.
The descent is so gradual that one scarcely seems to
advance downwards, and the length of time necessary
to accomplish it (upwards of an hour) will give some

3

idea of the vastness and grandeur of the scene. Continuing on, the gorge opens to the south, where the streamlet of the Curral, joined by several lateral branches, forms the River Socoridos, which empties itself into the sea at the ancient town of Camera de Lobos."

Funchal, off which the "Celt" anchored, is the capital of the island. It consists of a pretty wide street along the sea shore, where there are several good buildings, and small lanes extending from this street to a considerable distance up the slope of the hill. There are about 2,000 houses, inhabited by about 20,000 people. The place is defended by four forts, and has eight churches and several convents. In the midst of the town is an open square, planted with exotic trees. The view of Funchal from the harbor is very pleasing; its situation, in a kind of amphitheatre formed by the mountains, adds to its beauty. The contrast of the white buildings and villas with the green mountains forms a picture which is much heightened by the bold quadrangular Loo Rock, with its embattled summit commanding the harbor in the foreground. The most conspicuous objects on the west side of the bay are the peak of Ponta da Cruz, the Pontinha, with the Loo Rock near it, and the old Fortress of the Pico, on a rocky eminence half a mile north of them. Eastward of these are the Castle of Lourenzo, the official residence of the governor; on the beach and the outlet of the San Paulo River, the square towers of the ex-Jesuit College, the Cathedral, having a small triangular spire, Bangor's Pillar, on the beach near the Custom-house ; and on the extreme east, the Castle of Santiago, with the quintas upon the sloping land behind it. All these buildings are very conspicuous and of dazzling whiteness. In the background, casting the eye far up the terraced streets, in the midst of rich and luxuriant verdure, almost touching the clouds with its white towers, appears the highest and most striking building of all, that of the convent of Nostra Senora de Monte. This stands out conspicuously on one of the mountain ridges, which descends from the Peak of Arrebentao towards the city. The convent is 1,965 feet above the sea, while the peak itself is 3,844 feet high.

The gardens in the vicinity of Funchal are extremely beautiful, abounding as they do in trees, shrubs and flowers, and so many varieties of delicious fruits and vegetables common to the tropics and to Europe or America. The markets are in consequence well supplied with these good things, and all necessary refreshments.

The chief export of the island in former years has been wine, or the juice of the grape, which grew in greatest perfection here ; and this is where the genuine " Madeira wine," known the world over, is produced. But of late years the grape culture is said to have been a failure, and, in consequence, many of the inhabitants are poor. Most of the people are of Portugese extraction. Having procured a basket of fruit, consisting of oranges, lemons, Madeira nuts, chestnuts, bananas, apples, etc., at six o'clock we were again on board the ship, wearied with the haste, labor, and excitement of so rapid a survey of so much of the grand and beautiful of

Nature's charms, heightened by the presence and skill of man. Before leaving the subject, I may say further, that many of the poorer classes of the inhabitants endeavor to earn their subsistence by making baskets of cane or reeds, and also chairs and walking-sticks. They weave the baskets and chairs very beautifully, and the large, easy chairs they construct must be both comfortable and ornamental for a seat upon the lawn, and they are very cheap.

At about seven o'clock the engine shafts were again set in motion, the sails were hoisted, and the ship's prow began again to divide the waters on her course to the southward. After Madeira and its people had received their due share of our attention, and each passenger had recounted his or her adventures on her shores, the next subjects of conversation and anticipation were the tropics, which we were swiftly approaching. On Tuesday, January seventeenth, the following day after leaving Madeira, my diary says we were "wafted along by a steady and gentle breeze towards the Cape of Good Hope," and that it was "a very fine summer's day;" indeed, after leaving the cold and biting frosts of the north, and taking in its place this mild and invigorating breeze of the sea, in the temperate clime where we now were, my spirits felt renewed; and the heart that had been sad and lonely would almost, from the soothing breath of the air, rebound with joy and gladness. The world is yet beautiful; and if the sun withdraws his rays, or sends them obliquely, with chilling winds and blighting frosts, to one portion of the earth, it is only that he may shine more brightly and with greater

splendor on another portion. It is only in compliance
with the great law of nature and of God, often imitated
by the actions of men—what is given to one is withheld
from another, and this must be the great law of the
universe. Every thing around us, as well as every
sense and experience, shows that where darkness reigns
the sun cannot shine, and where the sun shines darkness
cannot reign. One giveth, and another receiveth. One
farmer tills the rich soils of nature, and receives an
abundant harvest; another takes up his abode on the
barren rocks or sandy plain, and attempts to force his
bread from the unyielding earth. The merchant in-
vests his means, and from some cause at the end of a
year finds his capital wasted, while his neighbor lays up
a store of wealth in the same period of time. Two
youths set out on the journey of life; one climbs the
hill of fame, and honors seem to shower upon him, while
the other only travels the humbler walks of life. The
history of the world tells the same tale; one nation falls
and perishes, and another rises to fill its place. Babylon and Thebes sink into decay, and Athens and Greece
rise. Greece and Carthage declined, while Rome, in
all her power and magnificence, became ruler of the
world. Rome is crushed beneath the burden of her
wealth, luxury, power, and the weight of years, and all
the modern great nations of Europe raise their heads
from off its ruins. If there is a more beautiful world
than this, we certainly, while living here, do not enjoy
it, and if we ever do, we shall have to leave this world
with all its attractions before we can wing our flight to
its blissful abodes.

On the second day after leaving Madeira the Canary Islands could be seen by us in the distance on the east side of the ship. These islands also seemed very mountainous, as viewed from the decks of the "Celt." The highest peak, called Pico do Teyde, on the Island of Teneriffe, was covered by clouds while seen by us early in the morning. It is over 12,000 feet high (12,180), and when the weather is clear it is said it can be seen upwards of one hundred miles. The following description of this mountain, given by a visitor several years ago, may interest the reader: "From our anchorage we had been daily tantalized with a glimpse only of the very summit of the Peak, peeping over a nearer range of mountains, and the hazy state of the weather on the day of our departure made us fearful we should pass on without beholding any more of it; but towards sunset, when we had reached some miles from the coast, we were most agreeably disappointed by a fair view of this gigantic cone. The sun set behind it, and as his beams withdrew, the mountain was thrown forward, until it appeared not half its real distance. Then followed a succession of tints and shades, from the glowing colors of a tropical sky to the sombre purple of the deepest valleys, varying in intensity with every intermediate range, until a landscape was produced which, for beauty of outline and brilliancy of color, is rarely surpassed." These islands, of which Teneriffe is the largest, are the native homes of the little canary birds that have become pets and songsters in so many households. The first mate of the "Celt" took on board at Madeira—where they are taken to market—a large cage full of these warblers for his friends in the south.

It now became evident that we were approaching the trade winds of the equator. In the afternoon of the day last named the sea became very calm and smooth, which is called the calm belt between the northern winds and the trade winds. The sun came out bright and warm, all the sails of the ship were reefed, and noiselessly the steamer glided through the water, dashing the spray over her prow as she moved swiftly along. Here was the first calm of the ocean I had seen, and again admiration, wonder, and pleasure filled the heart. The solitude that reigns around!—the quiet beauty of the glassy waters!—you start at a point in the horizon and survey its boundaries, a perfect circle, till the eye again reaches the point of departure—the sea and the sky meet on all sides, the ship with her precious burden is the whole world for the hour, and the sun above seems to shine only for the lone vessel. "Yet in this stillness there is a solemn sound, a voice that speaks in measured tones." Such scenes must awaken an eloquent tongue and inspire the artist's pen.

"Lies a calm along the deep,
Like a mirror sleeps the ocean,
And the anxious steersman sees
Round him neither stir nor motion.

"Not a breath of wind is stirring,
Dread the hush as of the grave
In the weary waste of waters,
Not the lifting of a wave."

One day crossing this belt of calm sea, and the next we caught the breeze of the trade winds, and all the sails were set and the ship flew more swiftly along. About this time large numbers of flying fish were seen skimming along out of the water before the vessel, as though frightened from their element. They would rise from the sea, fly sometimes a long way, and then drop into it again. In the evenings several of them, doubtless attracted by the lights of the ship and flying across her course dropped on deck, and were picked up by the sailors and cooked and eaten by them. Their bodies were much like an ordinary small fish from eight to ten inches in length, with quite long pointed wings, their color deep blue, like the sea. Occasionally, also, we would here see shoals of porpoises, a very large, dark fish, sometimes called the sea hog. They would shoot along near the side of the ship, sometimes showing their bodies above the surface of the water. One of the passengers shot one of them as it rose from the water near the vessel, but it could not be obtained.

As we neared the line of the equator, the atmosphere became very hot, the sun at noon was almost perpendicularly over our heads, sending his burning rays down unmercifully upon us. Canvas was stretched across above the upper deck of the ship as a shade, by the obliging officers, who, I believe, endeavored to make the passengers as comfortable as possible, and reclining under the shade, with the cooling breeze created by the motion of the steamer, fanning the person with its delicate softness, one can easily imagine how the inhabitants of the land in such a luxurious climate became enervated and sluggish.

It has been the custom among sailors "so long," as the lawyer hath it, "that the memory of man runneth not to the contrary," whenever any adult person on board their ship is " crossing the line " or the equator, for the first time, to "shave him," unless he furnishes champagne, and among some crews the intended sport is carried to the height of cruel barbarity. After having the capillary protuberance of his face properly eliminated by a competent esculapius, he is politely secured with a line, handed over to the mercies of the deep; and this is sometimes carried so far as with another rope to haul the subject under the ship and out upon the other side, called keel-hauling; and there have been cases in which the poor man has perished while undergoing this exercise. But, of course, such fun is not allowed on a line of passenger ships; yet as many of the passengers had before crossed the line and a number had not, among them the theme was fully discussed, pro and con, which resulted in the sailors faring much better, no doubt, than they would if permitted to perform their ancient rights.

Soon after crossing the equator, the trade winds were adverse to the course of the ship, and all her sails were consequently furled, the fore and main top-sails were taken off their yards and lowered into the store-room, and the fore and main yards lowered even with the upper decks, and the vessel put in proper trim to make all possible headway against the wind which was expected to blow with a steady force against our course during the rest of the voyage; and now all the power of the engines was forced to work, and still we were driven swiftly on our way. Of the trade winds it may be said, the effect of heat upon the air is to expand its

3*

volume. Winds are the consequence of a disturbance
of the equilibrium of the layers of the atmosphere,
and the tendency of these aerial currents is to restore
the equilibrium which has been destroyed; when the
density of the air is diminished by heat, it is specifi-
cally lighter than it was; as a consequence the warmer
body of the atmosphere must rise when pressed upon
by the cooler and heavier masses contiguous to it. Also
we must remember that the land is heated more
readily than the sea or an island; in proportion as the
sun rises above the horizon the land becomes warmer
than the neighboring sea, Their respective atmos-
pheres participate in these unequal temperatures, and
after sunrise the sea breeze springs up increasing in
strength till two or three o'clock in the afternoon, when
it gradually dies away, and at sunset a perfect calm
prevails. During the night it is reversed as the land
cools more quickly than the sea, its atmosphere becomes
heavier and flows seaward as a land breeze.

These alternating air currents are prevalent on all
coasts within the tropics, where they occur every day
with great regularity, but in general, however, do
not extend either seaward or over land to any great
distance from the shore. What takes place on a small
scale, as just stated, passes on a larger one between an
entire continent and the ocean, or between the tropical
regions on the one hand and the temperate and polar regions on the other.

To the difference in temperature, unequal in dura-
tion and amount, correspond, as a consequence, particular atmospheric currents. To the difference of tem-

perature between the tropics and the poles, we owe the
trade winds, the great annual breeze, the constancy of
which is only the expression of the permanent inequality
of the distribution of solar heat.

In the hottest zone of our earth a constant current
of warm air rises over land and sea; this is replaced
from below by the colder air which presses in from
higher latitudes, from north and south, on both sides
of the equator. The air that has mounted up, warmed
and expanded, cannot go beyond certain limits, and
therefore flows back in the upper regions on both sides
toward the poles, and falling as it is gradually cooled
in its progress, it reaches the earth again in the middle
of the higher latitudes. The immediate effect of this
constant circulation of the atmosphere is the phenome-
non of the trade and counter trade, or as Sir John Her-
schel has it, anti-trade winds. The trades are winds
blowing from the poles to the equator, with their direction modified by the rotation of the earth on its
axis. In the temperate regions of the earth we are
accustomed to recognize the astronomical seasons,
spring, summer, autumn and winter. But seasons of
temperature are unknown between the tropics. The
seasons here are regarded by the inhabitants only as
the rainy and dry. When the trade wind (N. E. or S. E.)
blows with its accustomed regularity, the sky preserves
a constant serenity, and is of a deep azure blue; the
atmosphere is then perfectly dry and cloudless. This
is generally the case when the sun is in the opposite
hemisphere; and as the sun approaches the zenith of
any place, the trade wind blows more irregularly, giv-

ing place to variable winds, the sky assuming a whitish tint, and becomes overcast and cloudy, and in the afternoon, when the heat has attained its maximum, a storm, with heavy showers, ensues, pouring down at times in a perfect flood of rain, inundating the earth with torrents of water.

At this period, the air is so moist that, in many places —between the tropics, the inhabitants live, as it were, in a kind of vapor bath—the heat is oppressive and stifling, the body is completely enervated, and the mind grows dull and listless. This is the time when those fevers that destroy so many of those reared in a temperate climate, is prevalent. But it is also the season when vegetation puts on new freshness and vigor. Ere long the sun in his annual progression advances to pour down his vertical rays upon other places, and the rains diminish, the air becomes once more serene, the sky clear, the trade wind resumes its regularity, and the rainy season is over.

On the morning of February 2d, the "Celt" anchored off the Island of St. Helena, a barren, solitary rocky island, standing alone. with the tops of its naked mountains rising high above the sea. It is said no coast in the world presents such a chilling appearance as this island, with its steep and cloven crags, its rocky ridges and fearful fissures, and no one beholding this forbidding shore can imagine the island contains some beautiful scenery. Approached from the northward, it has the appearance of one vast rock or castle, surrounded by the sea, its shores being high, rugged, and precipitous. But as you get nearer, the prospect somewhat improves,

the mountains are distinguished by different hues, and
the verdant tint of their summits is made out, varied
with the green hills and valleys of the interior. The
town next comes into view; situated in a narrow valley between the mountains, and with the churches, the
batteries, and white houses, interspersed with trees, form
quite a picturesque scene. The island is situated in
south latitude 15° 55', longitude west 5° 43' about 1300
miles W. N. westward of Port Alexander, the nearest
port on the African continent, 1,700 miles N. N. westward from the Cape of Good Hope, 1,320 miles N.
N. eastward from Tristan da Cunha, 1,750 miles S. eastward of Cape San Roque in Brazil, 1,900 miles eastward of Cape Trion, and 700 miles southward of As-
cension Island, the nearest land. So it can be seen
the English did not intend Napoleon I. should walk
away from their control easily. The form of the island
is nearly that of a parallelogram nine miles in length
and six miles in width, and contains an area of about
30,000 acres

The altitudes of the most prominent peaks of its
mountains, as reported by Major Rennell, are Diana's
Peak, 2,692 feet above the level of the sea; Cuchold
Point, 2,672 ; and Halley's Mount, 2,467. These form
part of a ridge running from the middle towards the
west, and are frequently enveloped in clouds. Flag-
staff Hill, near the northern shore, attains an elevation of 2,272 feet ; Sandy Bay Ridge, on the south,
2,215 ; Long Wood House, near the centre, 1,762 ; and
Lot and Lot's Wife, in the southwest, 1,444 and 1,423
feet respectfully. So it can also be perceived that the

English, with their tender care, kept their exiled prisoner as high up in the world as was consistent, thinking, doubtless, his elevation in height, would, in some
degree, compensate for his fall in power.

The general character of St. Helena is neither that
of beauty nor fertility; the few verdant places in it de-
rive a brighter appearance from the gloom and naked-
ness that prevail around them. The lower strata of
the island are mostly of a dark brown color, and have
every appearance of volcanic formation, and volcanic
productions have been found in all parts, leaving no
question as to its origin.

The geological formation consists almost entirely of
basalt, over which, in some parts, are strata of lime-
stone, mingled with tufa and other igneous substances.
The only feature, however, at all resembling an extinct
volcano is a deep crater-like dell, called the Devil's
Punch-bowl.

As soon as the ship came to anchor and permission
was given, I put off in a small boat for Grahamstown,
the capital. As we were allowed only about six hours
upon the shore, it was necessary that I should make all
haste, as above all else it was desirable to make a pilgrimage to the tomb of the great conqueror, Napoleon
Bonaparte, and to Longwood House, his exiled place of
residence. Ascending James' Valley from the town
at its mouth, we arrived at the Plaisa of Longwood, situate in the eastern part of the island and nearly 2,000
feet above the sea, sloping gently towards the south-
east. Longwood House still stands and presents a
very picturesque scene, surrounded by trees and the

verdant plains stretching away with the blue sea meeting the horizon in the far distance, and it is a place to fully impress upon one the solitude of its position, and its great distance over the boundless ocean from the world of nations.

Napoleon when defeated at Waterloo, deserted by by his friends, and opposed in the councils of his country, had thrown himself on the generosity of the commander of a British man-of-war, and taken refuge on board his vessel. He soon after learned that he would receive the same treatment as a general of the French army, and be held as a prisoner of war. When the government of Great Britain learned that they had him in their power, it was determined in the councils of that nation to carry him a prisoner to the Island of St. Helena, which then, as now, was a dependancy of that country. Therefore, in the autumn of 1815, Napoleon was landed on the island, where he remained under the strict surveillance of the English soldiery till he died, May 5th, 1821. The French government at the time of his death being under another dynasty hostile to his family, permission to carry his body to France and bury it there, as he had requested or desired, " on the banks of the Seine, in the midst of the French people whom he so much loved " could not be obtained, and his remains were consequently entombed on the island, near Longwood House which had been his residence. In 1841 his ashes were carried to France and buried with great pomp and splendor. Ever since St. Helena became the residence of this illustrious and at last unfortunate man, it has assumed an interest and attraction which few, if any, islands possess.

Situated as it is in the midst of the sea all alone, the traveler, after a long voyage, is glad even to set his feet again upon the solid earth, and especially when he can meet with objects of historical interest that call up the lives of the great, and call back the revolving years that have swept them away, even as the lowliest. St. Helena has now about five thousand inhabitants, one-third of which are Europeans, and the rest blacks, men of color, Chinese, etc. Its climate is considered one of the healthiest under the tropics, yet it is not considered healthy as a place of residence for Europeans.

The inhabitants of Jamestown seem to depend mostly for their means of subsistence upon trade with the vessels that for any cause may anchor off the town, and since the opening of the Suez canal, their business has been considerably cut off on account of the East India traders, many of them passing that way. Many of the people are very poor and said to be growing poorer daily, and are leaving the island.

At noon the strolling passengers were again called aboard the ship, and soon thereafter she was pushing her way over the sea, past the eastern side of St. Helena, which, before nightfall, had settled down in the northern horizon out of view from her decks, and we now looked forward to the Cape of Good Hope and to the termination of our voyage.

CHAPTER III.

On Sunday the 12th day of February, about noon, land again came in view on the southwestern coast of Africa. Towards evening, Table Mountain became distinctly visible, covered, as it was, with a white cloud; at seven o'clock the steamer came to anchor in Table Bay, with a salute of two cannon, answered by the fort at Capetown. Early Monday morning she entered the docks, and commenced discharging her cargo, while the passengers went ashore, many of whom were only booked to this place. But this line run their steamers to Algoa Bay, and I had paid my passage to that place on the representation of the agents in London, that it was the best place to land if going to the Diamond Fields. However, as soon as we arrived in Cape Town, I learned that there was an express wagon leaving this place once a week for the Fields, that it performed the journey in from seven to ten days, and that there was no such accommodation from Port Elizabeth, travelers from that place being compelled to provide their own conveyance, or take the slow ox wagons that were from thirty to sixty days in reaching the "diggings." This information was fully confirmed, and such was the case at the time I left the country, having traveled over both routes.

I consequently determined to leave the ship here and take passage to Cup Drift by the Inland Transport Company's express wagon that was to leave Cape Town for the Vaal river on the following Thursday. After securing my ticket for this journey, which cost me £12, having three days of leisure, I employed the time in seeing the sights and viewing the scenery in and about the metropolis of South Africa.

Cape Town is situated in south latitude 33° 56', longitude east 18° 28', and in the southwest corner of Table Bay, at the foot of Table mountain, and between it and the Bay it is regularly laid out, contains several good squares, and the streets, which are straight and wide, cross each other at right angles, many of them being watered by canals, and planted on either side with trees. The buildings are chiefly two stories in height, and are constructed with flat roofs in consequence of the violent winds to which the place is subject; they are built of stone, the exterior being white-washed or neatly stuccoed. The interiors are spacious and convenient, and many of them have terraces or steps before them, frequently shaded by a small row of fir trees which form an agreeable relief to their dazzling whiteness, and afford the advantage of a shady walk. The terrace walks in front of the houses are generally the favorite lounge of the family in the evening or during the heat of the day, and at all times affording an agreeable promenade. The Heerengracht or Gentlemen's Walk is the principal and fashionable street of the town. Some of the banks and stores, or warehouses, are constructed with considerable beauty of architecture.

The city contains about twenty-five thousand inhabitants, and has its parks and parade grounds, as well as its
public flower-gardens, and a museum containing an extensive collection, especially of African curiosities and
of fishes from the southern seas, together with a large
library open to the public. The governor of the colony, which belongs to England, resides at this place, and
the government buildings are here, and the Cape Parliament is held in this city. The principal public buildings are the Government House, with extensive gardens, the Burgher Senate House, barracks, Commercial Exchange, Custom House, Military depôt and Tax
office; English, Dutch, Lutheran and Presbyterian
Churches; Roman Catholic, Independent Wesleyan,
and Missionary Chapels; Somerset and other hospitals;
a theatre, Freemason's lodge, South African College, etc.

Cape Town is the seat of the Supreme Court of Justice for the colony, the Vice-Admiralty Court, and a
court for the recovery of small debts; and among the
banks there are several Savings institutions; it has several public free schools, and many literary, scientific,
religious, and benevolent associations, and a large and
elegantly-constructed observatory, situate about two
miles from the town. The only railroad in the colony
is built from Cape Town to Wellington, a distance of
fifty-eight miles. The English soldiers are also gar-
risoned at Cape Town; but England, I am informed, is
carrying out the same policy with Cape Colony as with
many of her other foreign possessions, and withdrawing
her troops and military aid, and leaving each dependancy
to raise, train, and pay its own soldiers.

The greatest attraction in nature near Cape Town is Table Mountain, which rises to an elevation of upwards of three thousand and five hundred feet (3,582) above the sea, and on the top is perfectly flat, and is frequently covered with a "blanket" as it is called, a white cloud which will hang over its sides like a cloth, exhibiting strikingly the appearance of a table on a large scale, with its white linen cover. As seen from the town, the mountain appears to rise just back of the city, and the stranger would think its top to be only a short walk from the place; yet the distance is twelve miles. Its height and greatness when viewed from the ship lying at anchor in the bay, made the white buildings of the town, by comparison, look very low and flat, like little play-houses. The mountain rose up before you bold and grand, and as the beholder gazes at its lofty sides and even outline, and thinks of the revolving years in which its granite walls and firm foundations have stood unshaken by the hand of time, and will stand for ages on ages yet to come, while everything that man is able to construct but endures for a few years and then fades away, like the morning dew or withering flowers, it cannot but lead him to contemplate that there is and must be a Great, Divine, and Omnipotent Architect whose hand is here visible, and who has here erected a monument to his glory, to remind his children of his power and will to create for their pleasure. These thoughts may be those of the middle-aged contemplative mind, when for the first time looking upon some of the great works of nature as exhibited on the surface of the earth. And why should we not elevate our minds from the contemplation of things great and wonderful on earth to still higher and nobler objects, to heaven which it is said is to endure even longer than the eternal hills, *forever!* aye, forever! Though the earth were all one solid rocky mass, and an immortal sparrow should strike its surface with her tiny little wings once every hour till it wear it away out of existence, still, forever, eternity means yet more time—if you wish, would have but begun.

But I hear the reader calling me back to the theme of my book, and perhaps I had better not weary his or her patience with a lengthy description of the other objects of interest to be seen in and about Cape Town.

The stranger will visit the museum where hours can be spent with pleasure, viewing the animals taken in Africa and the Southern ocean, and the statues of the different native inhabitants of the country and their weapons of war. Also the gardens just back above the museum, where the native plants and trees are grown. Before leaving the city the fruit market should be mentioned. I arrived in the midst of the fruit season, and it was very plentiful and very cheap. Two large bunches of beautiful white grapes, upwards of a pound, were only one penny, splendidly fine peaches and pears, two for a penny, and watermelons of the largest size for three or four pennies each.

The vine in the country about Cape Town is cultivated to a considerable extent, yielding, for export, wine and raisins.

Thursday morning, February 16th, commenced my journey by land to the Diamond Fields. Taking the

cars at the station in Cape Town, where also the wagon
was put on a platform car, at a quarter past seven
o'clock the train moved out of the depot, and we were
off for new scenes again.

It was a very pleasant and beautiful morning; the
air was warm, yet refreshing, and as the engine gave its
whistle and the train went rattling away into the country, we felt we had hardly yet left civilization behind;
and when, as we passed along, we could look out and
see the toiling farmer in his fields, the growing vineyards, and nurseries and orchards of fruit trees, and now
and then a small village or hamlet, with its white cottages clustering at the foot of some gently sloping hill,
verily it was a sight beautiful to see; and after the long
voyage upon the waste of waters, it was cheering to
look out upon the green earth again, with its trees, its
shrubs, its flowers, and its vines.   All around, the
verdure looked new and fresh; and with the balmy
morning air fanning the cheek, and the birds singing
among the trees, one could but think of home, and
how much like it this land seemed.

But ere nightfall, I am sorry to say, the delusion was
all past, and, I fear, buried forever out of the imagination.   In about three hours after, stopping at little ham-
lets on the way, the train reached Wellington, the ter-
minus of the railway. One could hardly conjecture why a
railroad should be required from Cape Town out to this
little place; but probably the enterprising people of South
Africa wanted a railroad, and as this was the best they
could do, they gave the place a big name, thinking perhaps that would offset against its size, and built their road

out to it—a very laudable affair, especially as payments were made with foreign capital, or money procured in England. When the cars stopped, the transport wagon was taken off, eight fine, spirited horses, two abreast, attached to it; the passengers took their seats, and before a loud crack of the whip, the team started off on the full jump. The wagon contained four very comfortable seats, and a smoking seat behind. There were on this occasion ten passengers, two drivers, and the guard or conductor, making three on a seat and the guard behind, and at first sight there was the prospect of a jolly as well as rough time before us.

The horses were full of life and animation, and started off in grand style. Leaving Wellington at about eleven o'clock A.M., our course soon began to wind around the base of a mountain range; and as the road gradually ascended the sides of the rising land, some of the most extensive landscape I had ever beheld was spread out to view before us. As far as the eye could extend its powers of vision, over the undulating plains below for many miles, and up to the very base of the mountain over a thousand feet beneath us, it looked like a vast uncultivated farm—at one point a clump of trees or shrubs, then a cleared spot like pasture lands, some places being barren and with a reddish tinge, as though the soil were uncovered; and here and there, separated by several miles, stood now and then a lonely dwelling. During all the day we were winding up and around the sides of mountains; at some points we could look up above thousands of feet before the eye rested on their tops, and at some places, over the protecting wall of the narrow road, thousands of feet below into a great chasm, at the bottom of which a little stream of water ran down its narrow bed. Sometimes the road would suddenly turn at an angle in the mountain side, and the leading horses would dash around it with great speed, while the clash of the driver's whip would ring far away in the gorges : it was indeed exciting and thrilling.

The magnificent scenery before us, beautiful and grand beyond the pen of the artist to delineate or the power of the orator to portray ; the rocks and hills above; the sloping mountain side below; the extensive country spread out before us; the narrow road, in whose crooked path the spirited horses were guided with the skiil of an experienced driver, who, proud of his autho- rity, would often rouse their mettle, especially in turn- ing sharp corners, with the loud clap of his long whip— all made it a scene to be looked on and enjoyed but once in a lifetime. Passing up and through the moun- tains all the day, till, as the sun began to disappear be- yond the western ridges, we came out on a fertile plain, and soon after, about seven o'clock, entered the little vil- lage of Ceres, a hundred miles from Cape Town, which we had left in the morning. Here a good supper of roast fowl, boiled eggs, vegetables and fruit, awaited us at the inn kept by a jolly Dutchman, and six hours were allowed for sleep.

At two o'clock the next morning, being aroused when the wagon was ready to proceed, and having taken our seats, we were again, with fresh horses, dashing swiftly over the road, traveling till about nine A.M. over an- other range of mountains, when we arrived at a station called Karoo Poort, where breakfast was provided, and another team of ten mules were inspanned. Karoo Poort is an opening between two mountains, being an even, level passage out on to a country called the Karoo, more fully the Karoo Plains, a most desert tract, without water or forage for man or beast for upwards of forty miles, and in whose centre can be seen, rising on all sides in nearly a circle round it, the ridges of the lofty mountains.

At ten o'clock (Friday morning, February 17th, 1871), the little team of ten mules commenced their even jogging trot through the Karoo Poort, out, on and over this plain, indicating by their paces that they knew the long and tedious day's work that was before them. The passengers, seeing the monotory of the road, after a short time settled back in their seats, with an attempt to make up for lost sleep the past night by dozing off their drowsiness as they jogged along.

Soon after the wagon had passed the Poort and had fairly got out on the plain, one of the passengers cried out, "See the Karoo porcupine; get out your pistols; we will get quite near before he will run, and you can get a shot." Most of us were at once straining our eyes to see a porcupine, especially a Karoo porcupine, which, as it was pointed out near the road ahead, appeared large and white, with great bones sticking up and out in different directions. Every one seemed so interested in trying to get a fair sight of the animal that fire-arms were entirely forgotten, and if it had been a carnivorous beast, dangerous to man, perhaps he might have destroyed us all before he could have been shot.

4

But the day of our death had not yet arrived, and as the wagon approached, we discovered the Karoo porcupine to consist of the bleaching carcass of an ox, horse, or mule, and afterwards, as we passed along, the bleaching bones of these dead animals could be seen strewn thickly on the plain near the road, and, in fact, all the way to the Vaal River; some which had just died, and others with nothing but the bones remaining. South Africa would be a good, or rather, an ample field for Mr. Bergh to make and enforce his law for the prevention of cruelty to animals. These poor beasts are driven here till, through exhaustion or the want of food or water, they drop down, when they are taken from the team, driven up and out of the road, and left to look for subsistence where there is none, and to perish. As soon as the breath leaves their bodies, the vultures and jackals attack them, and in a few hours nothing is left but the bleaching bones above mentioned. The journeys are long, the roads generally are poor, and the loads usually heavy; and even while at work the poor creatures get less food than when idle. Consequently, many of them die on the road; and in the interior, being cheap, when one fails its place is easily supplied, and, therefore, it is left often on the desolate plain to die of starvation.

After leaving Ceres, our journey was continued with but little rest, till we arrived at Beaufort West, on Sunday the 19th, at one o'clock P. M.—Friday night and Saturday night sleeping while sitting in the wagon, as we were riding along. Friday night, the other passengers said the driver was careless and sleepy, and they had to use all their pins and needles to keep him awake; that the wagon was nearly upset by his inattention a number of times, and they had not slept during the night. But not having heard of the dangers to which we had been exposed till the morning dawned, I had rested quite well, and during the day was awake to see the sights and enjoy the scenes of the country while passing along. And after drivers and teams had been changed, the others, doubtless feeling more secure, fell asleep; and it was fun to see them. One would let his head fall backward as though he would jerk it off; another one forwards; some one side, and some the other side. At first I could not help but laugh at their various oddities till the tears rolled down my face. But, begging their pardons a thousand times, I learned to see and indulge in such luxuries with respectable gravity, as we proceeded on our way. At Beaufort West we were allowed from one P. M. till two o'clock next morning for rest and refreshment; and all endeavored to make the best use of every moment of the time. First, a refreshing bath was provided and used, followed by clean linen. Then dinner; after which a short rest; then a little exercise, walking about the town; a light supper at seven P. M.; soon after to bed and to sleep, till the notes of the driver's bugle should wake us, when the small hours of the night began to strike the notes of another day.

I ought here to pay a proper compliment to two young ladies, daughters of the landlord of the inn at Beaufort West, for their kindness to us and their solicitude for our welfare while stopping there, and especially the elder one, who seemed to be a lady of the highest culture and refinement. I think none of the travellers expected to meet with such fair and accomplished ladies, so far in the interior of Africa, especially beyond the wild, uncivilized, uncultivated regions we had passed through, and it was exceedingly enlivening and cheering to converse and again listen to the charming conversation of such ladies. Their home, also, was well furnished and adorned with many luxuries, having, as one, a fine piano, on which they played with considerable skill and taste. With the charming society, and afterwards with the refreshing sleep that I enjoyed at this place, I passed a few of the pleasantest hours of my journey; and in the morning, when we departed, I found my lunch basket filled to the brim with pears, peaches, apples, and grapes of the finest quality. Beaufort West is quite a pleasant little hamlet, containing six hundred white people and about one thousand colored, and is situate upwards of three hundred miles from Cape Town.

Monday morning, February 20, at two A. M., the wagon again awaited us at the door of the inn, the guard endeavoring to awaken our drowsy minds with the blasts of his horn. All were quickly astir and climbing into the back, sides, or front of the heavy wagon, as was most suitable or convenient. The clash of the long whip is heard, and away we go out into the darkness, with the horses on the full jump, and with an occasional jolt that would wake a man up, if he was never awake before.

In such a journey, night and day, over rough and

uneven roads, and often with heedless drivers, if the traveller does not at first determine to trust his limbs and life in the hands of Providence, he will have a constant trial of his patience. On starting over this country I had fully made up my mind to let things take their course, and trust my good fortune for safety and health.

As we left Beaufort West, and at full speed rode out into a darkness where the leading horses could not be seen by any sense of vision I could bring to bear upon them, it would seem at any moment we were liable to be thrown out or overturned, with every chance of loss of health, if not of life. But we all settled back in our seats, preparatory to continuing our night's sleep as soon as the wagon was fairly under way, determined, if I may use a vulgar term, to "go it blind."

Our journey was kept up, with change of horses or mules, till ten o'clock P. M. of the same day, when we arrived at Victoria West, where another night's rest was allowed us.

This is also a neat little town, with its church, stores, and inn. The next day a Mr. Hanu, who had been one of the passengers thus far, and who was a merchant here, invited us to his residence and store, or winkle, as it is called in South Africa by the Dutch, and showed us several diamonds, among them one of fifty-six carats, of a yellow tinge, which he had recently procured from the Vaal fields. Mr. Hanu, all agreed, is as refined a gentleman as is seldom met—an open-hearted, whole-souled merchant—and it was gratifying to meet such a person, and to see him far in the interior

of this thinly populated country, surrounded with all
the comforts and many of the luxuries of life. One
would at first conclude, after leaving his home and place
of business, he was in the midst of a populous and refined people. Yet I believe I can safely hazard the
statement that there are not many men like him so far
up the country as Victoria West; and should any
reader pass that way and call on him, they will find a
genial and obliging man.

As the wagon was about leaving this town at one
o'clock, a heavy thunder shower for which the country
thus far north is noted, came on; for about one hour the
rain poured down, it would seem in almost one continual sheet of water, flooding the streets and roads, and after the rain had ceased, the lightning in the distant
clouds was very beautiful, the like of which is not to be
seen in more temperate climes. When the storm had
passed away the horses were again inspanned, and at
three o'clock in the afternoon our journey was continued with but little delay to Hope Town, on the bank of
the Orange river, at which place the wagon arrived on
the morning of the 24th of February. Plenty of wild
game was now seen from the wagon daily, often quite
near, consisting of springbok, spansbok, pows—
much like a turkey—and other birds. The teams between the two places last named were very poor, and it
was miserable work getting to Hope Town. The horses
on several occasions became completely exhausted and
refused to proceed; the weather during the day was
very hot, the sun sending down its vertical rays upon
the panting animals till they were nearly melted down

beneath its oppressive beams. Thursday evening, about ten o'clock, within seven miles of Hope Town, the poorly foraged horses became quite tired out, and totally refused to go on. The guard was obliged to order the driver to out-span and let them rest till morning.

The other passengers desiring to stay with the wagon, I concluded to walk on alone, and endeavor to get some rest at Hope Town before the wagon came up. I started about eleven o'clock in the night, and when first setting out could hardly see the road, and when there were paths in different directions, could not tell which to take, except to go straight on; so I journeyed on in the dark night, alone and afoot over seven miles of the desert plains, sometimes thinking a panther or wild cat was watching my course from among the clumps of low bushes scattered now and then over the plain.

Walking briskly for upwards of two hours, I began to hear the dogs bark; from which concluding I was on the right road, I hurried on, soon creating a general disturbance among the canine tribes as I entered the little village. Every household in the interior of Africa possesses its dog, and many of the Dutchmen have a number of these animals to guard their flocks and herds, as well as their doors and sheep folds. Seeing one house alight, while passing along, I made bold to summon its occupant to the door, from whom I learned the position of the village inn, where I was soon admitted by its hospitable host, and having told my story, was given a comfortable bed, on which with no delay I cast my weary body, and was at once securely folded in the arms of Morpheus, who held me fast

assisted by all his attendant angels, only yielding up
his power and flying away, long after the bright rays of
the rising sun had sent his golden beams with great
force against the head of the loving God, bidding him, in
language not to be disobeyed, that the hour for his departure had come, and he should no longer hold in
bondage a mortal whose days of toil were swiftly passing away.   Arising and assisting the sun in shaking off
the drowsy deity, I received the proper and needful
ablutions, sat down to and ate a hearty breakfast of
beef steak and mutton chops, soon after which the
wagon came dragging its slow course into the town
with the passengers straggling along.   The horses
were at once changed, and with a much better team, at
nine o'clock A. M., we proceeded on the journey.   Crossing the Orange river on a punt or ferry-boat, we were
now in the Orange Free State, a sort of Dutch Repub-
lic.   Perhaps I ought to state that now the inland transport company have much better horses between Victoria West and Hope Town, than was driven there
when I passed over the road.   After passing the
Orange river, the roads lay over grassy plains of sandy
or a light loam soil, with little variation in the general
prospect.

On the night of the 24th, there being no fresh team
at hand, and no inn, we were obliged to sleep in and
around the wagon, on the ground, while the horses were
permitted to feed and rest.   Early the next morning
the wagon was again moving on, and at eight o'clock in
the evening arrived at Pniel on the southern bank of
the Vaal river in the Orange Free State; and this was

the end of our tour, having been nearly ten days on the road since leaving Cape Town, the distance being seven hundred miles. The same wagon had brought us the whole distance, and the same guard had conducted it. Teams had been changed twenty times, and drivers several times.

After leaving the mountain-ranges and entering on the Karoo up to the Orange river, the tops of the mountains, interspersed here and there in the plain, seemed to be of one level, as though at some distant day their highest points and ridges had been the surface of the level earth, and that the light soil between them had been washed away, making the intervening plains and leaving them standing—a vast pile of boulders and round stone, all of nearly the same height, with even, level tops, sometimes running along several miles in the same mountain.

There was not in the country over which we had passed the volcanic indications I afterwards saw going down to Port Elizabeth. Here, from Cape Town to Pniel, it had more the appearance of one time being covered with water and of having been washed by the billows of some great inland sea, which had left the scattering mountains standing as the remains of islands on its surface, and carried away with its departing waters the light earth between them to some other depository.

When we arrived at Pniel the miners and inhabitants were expecting the Governor of Cape Colony, who was at that time making a tour through his dominions, and especially to the Diamond Fields. As our guard

4*

did not blow his bugle to announce the approach of the passenger wagon, the people took it for the Governor's conveyance, and we rode into Pniel amidst the huzzas of the crowd, with banners displayed from tents, houses and triumphal arches in grand style; and as the wagon stopped in their midst and the passengers were getting out, the leading dignitaries of the place were looking at each one sharply to find some person to read a speech to, or shoulder and carry off. But as no one just at that time seemed disposed to accept the proffered honor, the citizens had to delay their further demonstrations of joy till the next evening, when the Governor actually met them and returned their acclamations of welcome. And each passenger, picking out his baggage, sought an inn where he could rest till Monday morning, when all expected to try their luck in the Diamond Fields.

CHAPTER IV.

DIAMONDS were first found in South Africa nearly two years ago (in 1869) on the northern bank of the Vaal River; but no particular stir or excitement about them was created until the large diamond, called the "Star of South Africa," was brought into market in the early part of 1870. There are many different stories told of the circumstances attending the first discovery and sale of this magnificent gem; but the most creditable is, that it was picked up on the surface of the ground at, or near, Clip Drift, by a Korranna, a native negro, and sold by him to a Dutch farmer, who gave all the sheep and cattle he possessed to the native for it. The farmer then took it to Sir Philip Wodehouse, the then Governor of the Colony, at Cape Town, who paid him five hundred pounds sterling for it, the farmer at the same time being instructed to dig for diamonds where they were found on the surface. The "Star of South Africa" has since been cut, and is now owned by and in possession of the Prince of Wales, and is said to be valued at thirty thousand pounds sterling.

After the discovery of this stone there was quite a rush of the scattered population of the country to the Vaal River and the hills in its vicinity, for the purpose of searching for these gems. This region then, especially between the Vaal and Heart rivers, was entirely

uninhabited, being a sandy, stony, hilly and barren tract
of land.   Digging for diamonds was first commenced
on a copay or rising elevation of land north of the Vaal
river, and near its bank, where it turns suddenly from a
south-westerly to a northern course, and where the town
of Clip Drift has since been built and grown into a thriving village.

These gems appear to have been mostly found on the
copays along the banks and in the ancient beds of the
Vaal.   When the Clip Drift copay was principally
worked out, the diggers began to search for new places,
and many crossed the river and commenced operations
at Pniel, which has since proved a very rich mine; also
Cawoods Hope, Gong-Gong, Bad Hope or Victoria, the
Colesburg copay, Sivenelle, Union copay, Natal copay,
Hebron, Diamondia ; and places called new rushes, up
and down the river from Clip Drift and Pniel, on either
side, were opened and being worked when I left the
fields, in April last (1871) ; and also Du-Toits-Pan,
Bell Fontaine, and other farms, miles away from the
river, were proving quite rich in the precious stone, at
that time and afterwards.

When it was reported in England that diamonds had
been found in this region of country, and that a vast
tract—in fact the whole wilderness about the Vaal and
Orange rivers—was supposed to be diamondiferous, a
geologist was sent out to the colony to make an investigation, and report as to the truth of the stories coming
from it.   This gentleman, after examining the soil and
earth supposed to contain diamonds, returned to England with the impression that it was not a diamond-pro-

ducing country, and made a statement of his investigation, arriving at the conclusion that the soil was not
diamondiferous, and that the reports printed and circulated to that effect were but delusions in the minds of
the inhabitants. Another would-be geologist, residing
in the colony, issued a book, or essay, in which he attempted to refute the arguments of the English miner-
alogist, and by facts and sound reasoning to establish
the truth that his opponent was wrong, and that diamonds were to be found and were found, and that the
hills and former river beds near the Vaal were a diamond-producing soil.

But while these theorists were wasting their time
and labor in such vain attempts to establish or dis-
prove the truth, as is usual in such cases, the strong
arm of the honest, industrious man of toil was working out proofs not to be denied. And it soon became
an established fact that these precious gems there existed, and were found in considerable numbers.

The Colony at once determined to make as much
out of the discovery as possible, and while perhaps
there was some truth in the reports published and circulated over the whole country, and from that, of course,
sent to England and reaching America, circulated in
those countries; yet, as has always been the case on
the discovery of mines of gold, or silver, or precious
stones, many of the stories were merely wild and un-
truthful rumors set afloat by thoughtless and careless
persons, or wickedly originated and set in motion by
interested parties, who then, and constantly ever since,
have endeavored to deceive the public about the coun-

try and the diamond-producing regions. As has been heretofore stated, the first accounts were published in the United States in August and September, 1870. And in the New York *Herald* in September an extract from the Grahamstown (Cape of Good Hope) *Journal* of the 12th of August was published, which gave a very truthful statement. It says :

"There certainly never has been such a stir in this Colony before, excepting in time of war. Every town and district in the Colony has sent its contingent to the army of workers at the Vaal Fields, and still the movement goes on. In May there were about one hundred men at the diggings. Before the end of June there were seven hundred, at the close of July there were over one thousand, and at present it is estimated that there are at the Klip Drift, Pniel, Hebron and Kuskamana Fields no less than two thousand men. When it is remembered that the European population in the Colony is scattered over a large surface, and at the best but small, and that distances here are very great, it will be understood that pretty strong motives must have been at work to occasion so large a movement. The discovery of the 'Star of South Africa,' now known at home, has been followed by that of other stones. * * * As the fields are in a country owned by no one who can substantiate his claim, there is no organization of labor, and there are no means of ascertaining the actual discoveries. Some keep their good fortune to themselves, and again there are cases in which a diamond is talked about until it becomes several diamonds. * * * Some parties

are known to have been very successful. * * *
As a matter of course, out of so large a number of diggers, many have been greatly disappointed. * * * "
Therefore the existence of diamonds and the certainty
that they were being found in this region, far in the
interior of Africa, becoming an established truth, no
matter what false representations were made, or how
exaggerated accounts were given, which any thinking
mind could not believe. Yet there was a chance to
secure the much coveted and glittering jewels, and
many, without counting the cost or considering from
what cause such great value is placed, and always has
been placed, upon diamonds, and being ignorant of the
labor required and deprivations to be borne in order to
secure them, even if at all successful, abandoned their
homes and good situations, especially in England, to
try their luck in the Vaal Diamond Fields; and at the
time I left them, in April, 1871, it was estimated that
in the different localities there were upwards of five
thousand laborers at work in the mines, besides many
who had tried their fortune having returned to their
homes, and then I do not think the number of workers
was increasing, some leaving about as fast as others
arrived. During the time I remained on the fields, in
March and April, I endeavored to gain all the information I possibly could about the number of finds and the
success of the diggers generally, having visited nearly
every locality then being worked, and worked myself
for upward of a month at Cawoods Hope, where quite
a number of large diamonds were found.

When the people first began to flock to these fields

to search for diamonds, the country about the Vaal, though it had been previously owned or claimed and occupied by the Orange Free State, or by different tribes of the native inhabitants of Africa, was then totally un-inhabited, and consequently without any form of gov-ernment, or means of enforcing law or preserving order. Therefore, as soon as a sufficient number of miners set-tled on any copay or in any particular locality, they would appoint a committee of three or five from among their number, who, for a small fee while employed on committee business, and under by-laws, rules and regu-lations which would be agreed upon, would grant licenses to the diggers, preserve order and punish of-fences, and by general consent the authority of these committees was respected; and, governed by their regu-lations, wherever they were constituted, all were very peaceable and orderly throughout the fields up to the time I left them; and no crimes nor offences of im-portance had been perpetrated on or among the people.

In a few cases for petty larceny or some minor mis-demeanors, punishments had been inflicted. There being no prisons or jails, the officers were obliged to re-sort to the primitive modes of punishment, and there had been a few cases of whipping, mostly of the na-tives, and one or two cases of putting white men over the river, which consisted not only of taking the indi-vidual condemned across the Vaal River in a boat, but also while on the way over giving him a severe duck-ing under the water, and landing him on the other side much exhausted from his many and long immersions. These methods of punishment appeared to be quite effective, the person once passing through them being known and remembered afterwards in all parts of the Fields. Order and the safety of goods and chattels therefore seemed to be better and more secure than even in more settled countries, where all the paraphernalia of the law has its full sway.

The people were honest and industrious in their labors, and all appeared to trust to their neighbor's honor and integrity, and things were left scattered about with less precautions against theft than is taken in towns and villages of civilized countries. It was no place for idlers, every one was working with great energy in search of his prize.

But since and after the fields became an established fact, the Orange Free State government laid claim to the territory, especially on the southern and western side of the Vaal River; and also Waterboer, a native chief and his tribe, claimed that the same country, or some part of it at least, belonged to them. This tribe of natives, on account of some previous wars between them and the Dutch settlers of the Free State in which the English colony of the Cape had taken part, was at this time under the protection of the British government. Consequently, in the dispute between the natives and the government of the Free State as to the ownership of the diamond-producing country about the Vaal, the colonial government naturally became interested and took a part. Thus arose the rumor that there was to be a war at or over the diamond fields.

The Free State government sent on its magistrates and officers to enforce its laws and to collect heavy taxes and licenses of the miners and shop keepers, who, under the circumstances of its being disputed territory, very justly refused to submit to or pay until the question of ownership was decided, and especially as they had already established a government which was collecting a revenue of its own. This unsettled state of affairs, and the threatening war cloud that rose over the thriving little settlements, induced Sir Henry Barkly, the new Governor of the Colony, about the 1st of March, 1871, to visit the various "diggings" and also the President of the Free State, for the purpose of endeavoring to procure a peaceable settlement of the disputed questions between the miners, the Free State, and the various native tribes. At this time Cawoods Hope, a large settlement on the south-western border of the river, twelve miles below Pniel, or twenty miles following the course of the stream, was threatened with a commando from the Free State, which had assembled in the fields near Pniel, to enforce the payment of licenses and taxes demanded from the inhabitants. Therefore the diggers of that place organized themselves into a military body, and called on the neighboring miners to aid them, if necessary, to repel the power and presumption of the Dutch government, and for a few days Cawoods Hope was turned into quite a military camp, training and drilling the recruits, and an aiding force came down the river from Hebron. But, as was generally supposed, from lack of bravery among the Dutch, and seeing the determination of the people, the commando did not advance, but kept their forces encamped on their own territory. In the meantime, the various

contending parties had consented to submit the matters
to a commission which had been agreed upon, and the
miners again went to work, or rather continued their
labors, which had scarcely been interrupted by the occasional military meetings and trainings to prepare for
defense when attacked. Also, when work was first begun at Pniel, the missionaries among the native tribes
endeavored to exact from the miners twenty-five per
cent. of the value of the finds, which demand was likewise resisted by the diggers; and from such causes, followed by the proceedings above related, war at one
time on a small scale appeared quite probable. After
agreeing to submit to an arbitration all the differences,
the Free State still kept its commando of one thousand
raw and undisciplined men in the field, until the British
police force arrived, and the Governor refused to proceed with the arbitration unless it was withdrawn, when
the President of the Free State ordered its dispersion,
and the volunteer soldiery sought their several farms
and homes. And now I believe the questions have been
amicably adjusted, the territory divided, the Free State
holding Pniel and the country on the southern side of
the Vaal, and Clip Drift and the North being under the
protection of the British, and governed by a magistrate
duly appointed by the Governor of the Colony, who holds
a regular court and exercises jurisdiction in both civil
and criminal cases. Thus much for governmental affairs at these Diamond Fields.

There is not any probability of, and the diggers never
anticipate any, serious trouble over the country. The
native tribes of Caffirs, Korannas, Hottentots, etc.,

negroes or colored people, have long since been conquered and exhausted by their various wars with the Dutch
and English; and the Free State have not the power to
successfully cope with the English in a trial of arms;
therefore questions will be settled about as the colonial government determine, while keeping in view all the
just claims and rights of the contending parties, so that
no foreign power intercedes.

Perhaps I have dwelt too long on this subject of the
government of a country of so little importance to other
nations; yet they are questions of the rights, safety and
security of the diggers, and on the supposition that the
reader has the same curiosity that led me to gather up
the facts, I have recorded them. And in dropping this
subject let it be said, that without doubt peace will continue to reign, and law and good order be constantly en-
forced by the even hand of justice at the Diamond Fields
of South Africa for many years to come, and so long as
they are inhabited, as at present, by the white race; and
a man may live there with as much safety and protection against lawless men as in any part of the world.

The people thus far having proven themselves to be
an honest and industrious community, and that class is
now too strong in their influence and control to allow
persons of reckless characters to supersede them.

The methods of searching, digging, and washing or
sifting for diamonds at the Vaal Fields are numerous,
depending on the strength or number of the party at
work, and also on the locality in which the work is being
done.

When an individual or a company have decided on a

spot in which to try their luck, the first thing to be done is to pitch a tent for a home, to procure the necessary tools, picks, shovels or spades, a crow-bar, sieves, and cradle and cooking utensils, etc. Some take these things from the Colony with them, but that is useless, for while I was at the Fields they could be bought at auction sales held two or three times a week at each of the principal settlements, for nearly one-half less than in any part of the Colony, and, in fact, I think full as cheap as at any place in the world. A bell tent, for which new and of the same size £4. 10s. was charged in the Colony, I obtained second-hand at the fields for £2., and it was nearly as good as when new; picks and shovels from three to five shillings, or one half their cost at colonial stores, and nearly all the necessary tools and implements could be procured at these sales at similar prices: and if not at the auction sales there are plenty of stores at Pniel, Clip Drift, Hebron, and other places, at which they are sold at very moderate prices, considering the high tariff paid for transportation.

Having secured these things, the digger next obtains a claim or piece of ground in which to commence work. Claims are to be obtained in three ways, either taking a new plot which has never been touched, or jumping, or buying the claim of another. Each person is allowed a certain number of square feet, surface measure, usually thirty feet square, or nine hundred square feet, and the miner can pre-empt such a lot in any new place, or if he finds a claim partially worked which has been neglected or abandoned a certain number of days, he may take possession of it, called jumping it, or he can purchase a

claim of another who has an established right thereto.
When the Pniel Field was yielding its best, claims were
sold there as high as £100 each, but no such price has
since been obtained in any locality, and when I left the
fields as many were given away as were sold.   As soon
as a plot of ground is secured, a license must be obtained from the proper authority to work the claim, and bea-
cons set up on it showing its number and boundaries.
The fee paid for a license was a fixed sum to be paid
each month, the amount varying in different localities
from half-a-crown (about sixty cents) to ten shillings
($2.50).   Each claim must be continually worked, or
picked in at least every third day, otherwise it would
be considered abandoned and liable to be jumped and
the owner to lose his rights.

Such were rules in operation when I was at the
"diggings;" as to their stability it is impossible to affirm,
being liable to be changed by the government or the rules
of the miners; and, besides, there are farms in the Free
State being opened to the miners, and in such places the
rules and charges will be somewhat determined by the farmer or owner of the land.   When two or more persons are
associated together in working, each one is allowed a
claim and a license, and after one claim is worked out,
the other or others can be worked if the party has remembered to pick in it, and complied with the laws in
force at the place.   Being now ready to commence
work, as before stated, the methods are different in
different places and with different parties.   In localities
along the Vaal the miner commences in his claim with
pick, crow-bar, and spade or shovel, throwing up five or

six cart-loads of the gravel and earth, then with his cart and oxen, horses, or mules, or hired team (for which one shilling sterling is usually charged per load) carts the stuff to the river bank; some, whose claims are near, carry it in bags on their backs or in pails, or wheel it in wheel-barrows. At the river the gravel is washed in a cradle, which is made of an oblong box, varying in size, usually from two and a half to three feet long, and about two feet deep, open at the top and at one end near the bottom; this is placed on rockers like a child's cradle, the bottom usually projecting a few inches at the open end. In this box are placed two, and sometimes three, sieves above each other, with a frame to each three or four inches deep, so that when in the cradle they are that far apart; and a space of about that depth is left between the bottom sieve and the floor of the cradle. The lower sieve, or first one placed in the cradle, is fine enough to hold any diamond or stone worth saving, the next one above it, if there are three used, is coarser and would only catch stones about the size of common peas; the top sieve, whether two or three are used, is very coarse, with holes from a half to three quarters of an inch in diameter, and is only intended to detain the very large gravel. In most of the cradles no more than two sieves are used, the coarse and fine. The sieves are made of wire or perforated zinc and properly secured in the box. At the opposite end of the cradle, from the mouth, a handle is fastened, consisting of a piece of board or plank nailed or screwed on to it perpendicularly, and is of sufficient length so a man can stand up and do the rocking. The cradle thus constructed is placed near the river's edge, with the rockers on a good foundation, a pail-full of the gravel and earth is put in to the top sieve, and with the pail one man dips up and pours the water on the gravel in the sieve, while another is rocking the cradle, and so on, until the coarse gravel in the upper sieve is washed quite clean, and the finer stones have gone through to the other sieve. At one glance it is seen whether or not a diamond is among the coarse stones in the first sieve. Fortunate the man who finds one there, and surely it would be "picked up." When the contents of this sieve is at once emptied on the ground, and the sieve again fill-ed with gravel to be washed, and the washing thus con-tinued till the lower sieve or sieves become nearly full of the finer stones, when the top sieve is taken off, and with a few more pails of water the gravel in the lower washed entirely free from earth, when they are both taken out and emptied on to the sorting table. This table is made of all sizes, and of different materials, and consists of anything making a plain surface which will hold the stones, and at which a person can sit and sort and dis-charge its contents. The gravel being thus washed and placed on the table, a man with a stool on which to sit, takes his place at the table, and with a scraper, a small piece of zinc two inches wide, and three or four inches long, with one edge straight, commences sorting. Spreading out a small quantity of the gravel with the scraper thinly on the table before him casting the eye over it, picking out the diamonds or pretty stones which he may wish to save, then scraping it off on to the ground. Sorting is done very rapidly. On first seeing the operation the quickness, and seemingly carelessness,

with which a large heap of the stones are looked over
and thrown away, one would think diamonds would certainly be missed, and when new beginners commence at
this branch of the business they spend a great deal of
time in carefully looking at and testing all the pretty
stones, and especially all those transparent, and the
crystals, of which there are many. Sometimes a small,
well-shaped, clear crystal will raise their hopes to the
highest pitch only to deceive, and amateurs will get excited and be running about to their more experienced
neighbors with these stones, to learn they have but a
crystal which is wholly valueless. But experience soon
teaches in this as in other things that precious gems are
not found nor obtained so easily as the worthless crystals. And as diamonds are not only seldom found and
with many difficulties, yet they also cannot be mistaken
when met with in the gravel spread out on the table,
though given but a single glance. One will seem to
stare at you like a brilliant eye from among its dark,
lustreless associates. Even so the gems of humanity;
one bright and spotless is but seldom found, and, wherever existing, the lustre of the soul shines out with such
brilliancy, its true nature cannot be mistaken.

After once picking up a diamond among his gravel,
the digger will have no hesitancy in deciding what are
and what are not, these beautiful gems, with as much
certainty of a truthful decision as can possibly be made
in any conceivable case where two things are in question, and I believe that to be with sufficient certainty.

Besides the above, there are other modes of labor near
the river; some do the washing on their claims, when
5

only one or two persons are working together, and have
no cart or team. Then two or more large tubs are
used, generally consisting of a wine cask sawed into
in the middle, making two tubs; these are filled
with water carried from the river to the claim, and the
gravel is washed in these tubs, in a common hand sieve,
sufficiently fine to hold any stone of value; the miner
fills the sieve, and with arms bared placing it in the
water in one of the tubs and shaking it round till most
of the earth is washed out, and then in the other tub
rinsing the stones quite clean, then emptying it on the
sorting table as in the other case of the cradle. Sometimes the process of dry sifting is performed before
washing. When the soil is dry much of the earth in this
way can be sifted out, leaving the gravel to require
much less washing, as when washing in tubs they become
filled with dirt; it is shoveled out, and they are again filled with water, and the work again carried on. Such is
the process near the Vaal river, or where water is
plentifully supplied.

But at Du Toit's Pan and other farms and places
where there is no water, dry sifting is wholly resorted to, and is usually performed with a single sieve square
or quadrangularly shaped, with one end attached to a
swing and the other with handles, or both ends with
handles, so as to be shaken by one or two men, when
the diamond-producing soil is placed in it retaining the
gravel as in the sieves in the other case, which is sorted
in the same way. In rainy weather the operation of
dry sifting cannot be carried on, while the stuff is wet.

From the above description it will be seen, that in

order to work with advantage in washing the gravel at
the river requires a team—oxen are the best—and cart,
with at least three men and five or six are better. When
there are only three men, the afternoon is usually employed in throwing up the gravel out of the claim ; in
the morning it is drawn to the river, and during the fore·
noon washed and sorted, two men washing with the
cradle, and the third sorting, and at noon the drawn
gravel is usually washed and sorted, when the men
again work in the claim. One person with his team and
two hired natives in this way get along very well. With
five or six men, the washing can be continued all the
day by three, while the others are working the claim
and getting the gravel to the river bank. Where a
single individual is at work alone, he has many ways
of getting on, the best and most independent being to
wash in tubs on the claim, but it is very slow and very
hard work; and, in fact, when regularly carried on the
work is very laborious in all its branches.

CHAPTER V.

I HAVE spoken of claims of gravel and earth, etc.
Doubtless it is proper that I explain what is meant by
these terms; in other words, explain the appearance of
the soil or substance in which diamonds are sought for
and obtained in South Africa. It is generally conceded,
I think, by geologists and mineralogists, that the formation and existence of diamonds is one of the inexplica-
ble works of nature which men have not yet been able
to comprehend. Although they can be destroyed or
analyzed, and the properties of which they are composed be determined, yet the process of nature in combining those properties and infusing the coloring matter,
so as to make the hardness of the diamond and
give them their beautiful shades of color, as yellow,
red, blue, green, pink, brown, orange or leaves them
white, clear as the purest drop of water, has thus far
baffled the ingenuity and skill of man to find out; and,
so far as I can learn, if the soils where these unrivalled
gems are found are examined with the view of gaining
light on the subject, it must but disappoint the geologist, and, if anything, add to the darkness that already
surrounds him on this point. Although other gems
and beautiful and transparent stones are found in the
neighborhood of the diamond, still the gem itself turns
up in the most curious places, and often when least ex-

pected. One digger will have what is termed beautiful
gravel, and expect to see a diamond among the pretty,
shining stones every minute of his labor, and find none,
while his neighbor has, as both think, unfortunately dug
into a mass of crumbling rotten-stone, and is carelessly
hurrying through it, when, Lo! a sparkling diamond of
thirty or forty carats glitters among the unsightly mass;
with a little sentiment, I may add seemingly, like some
selfish men, having taken the beauty from everything
around to increase its own lustre.

The channel of the Vaal River, through the country
where the diamonds are found, is a considerable of the
way bounded on either side by high stony and rocky
lands, hills or mountains, chiefly of a light red or gray
color, in some places being one mass of large, broken
rocks; in others, covered with smaller stones, as large
as or larger than one man can lift, with broken bits of
white stone or reddish gravel scattered about in spots.

Near the edge of the stream the exposed parts of
the rocks and stones are frequently quite black looking,
as though they had been burned like coal, possibly by
electricity, perhaps by lightning stroke. In some parts
the rising, high boundaries of the river descend precipi-
tately to its edge, while in others it recedes and rises a
distance back from the stream, leaving a low elevation
or copay between the hills and the river, and these
places have generally been found to contain diamonds.
The land is mostly very uneven along the river, and
consists of masses of stone imbedded among pebbles
and earth, and is covered with stone, broken rocks and
pebbles, with very little soil.

On the copays along the river, and also in perfectly
flat, low places, among the large rocks and stones, lie
the gravel and water-worn pebbles in which the diamonds are found. The crevices of the rocks and the
earth between the massive stones is filled with this
gravel, and as the stones are removed one side it is
thrown up with the spade or shovel into a heap to be
washed and sorted. Doubtless these places were some
time the bed of the Vaal River, and from that a person
might be led to conclude that the diamonds and water-
worn pebbles were deposited here by the current of the
stream, and consequently that there must be a place
higher up the river from which they had been washed
down. But such a theory is entirely disproved by
other diamond-producing localities, which never could
have been the bed of any river—for instance, the
Natal Copay, near Cawoods Hope, both of which
places have proved quite rich, especially in large gems.
Cawoods Hope is a low land between the hills and the
river, from one to two miles long, and from one hundred to two hundred rods wide, the hills rising up back
from the stream the last named distance, and coming
again near the edge of the stream at each end. The
Natal Copay, where a diamond of 107 carats and
smaller ones were found, is one of the hills back of the
upper portion of Cawoods Hope, and, I should think,
a mile from the river in a direct line, and from it to
the river is a narrow channel where, in case of a heavy
rain, the water would flow down to Cawoods Hope and
the river; and, although I will admit this copay is not
quite so high as some of the hills on either side of it,

yet I do not believe any one looking at it and the vast plain on the other side, will affirm that it ever could have been the bed to the current of any river. It could only have been constantly washed by water, when the whole country was covered with that element. Even if thrown up by volcanic action it must have, like its neighbors, risen out of some vast body of water, or else we cannot affirm, or account for, its ever being submerged beneath a flowing current. The Natal Copay is only a small place, and was principally worked out in the first days of the diamond excitement in this country by a party from Natal, who are said to have literally reaped a golden harvest and to have distributed to each one of the company a handsome fortune. The large diamond, I think, was found by a native, from whom they obtained it for a small reward, with the information that this was the place where he picked it up, and therefore here they went to work, with the result above stated.

At Cawoods Hope, also, quite a number of large diamonds have been found, one of about ninety-four carats, two or three of over eighty carats, some of fifty, sixty, forty, thirty, etc., down to small ones. As the size decreases, in all the diggings, the number increases in a regular proportion. At Cawoods Hope upwards of two thousand people have tried their luck, many of them to find it bad. The claims at this field were worked only from two to five feet deep, below which what the miners call pot clay existed, which was considered not to contain diamonds, some parties having worked a great quantity of it, and although it contained

gravel, found no gems. Gong-Gong, or rather the new
rush below Gong-Gong, is also a low land near the
river, like Cawoods Hope, but on the opposite side;
and Union Copay, below that again, is another high
land, like the Natal. The Pniel and Clip Drift Copays, though near the river, on opposite banks, are also
higher elevations. At Pniel the claims are worked upwards of twenty feet deep; at Clip Drift not so deep;
but now it must be remembered that many of the
places of which I am speaking have been nearly worked
out and almost abandoned for new places. In the
river there is occasionally a rocky island, some of
which have been worked and gems found on them.
But none of the islands had proved to be very attractive to the diggers at the time I came away.

At Du Toits Pan, which was a farm (and I will take
that place as a specimen of all the diggings away from
the river,) about twenty miles from Pniel, in the Orange
Free State, claims at first were only worked in the
alluvial soil, about one foot deep, a very light, dry, sandy
soil intermingled with fine gravel. Garnets are here found
in quite large numbers, even on the surface they can
be picked up ; the miners call them rubies, but at the
same time know they are but garnets. When only the
upper layer of earth was worked at first, small diamonds
were found quite numerously, nearly every one finding
more or less ; but they were so small and of so little value, that this place did not attract much attention
until April last, when the diggers here began to go
deeper into the earth, below the light soil, into a hard
white granite or gneiss, when larger stones where found,

and in May, at the time I left the Colony, it was proving very rich and very attractive, even beyond all precedent.

The surface at this place has much the appearance of an ordinary field covered with grass, being slightly undulating, and is the same for many miles about, now and then in the distance a single mountain or high hill rising up to make the country look more desolate and wild. Yet in some spots the scenery is very beautiful and extensive. Below the foot or so of light soil in this field the deposit was very hard and compact. Clayey granite, quite white, intermixed with particles of gravel, the hard earth requiring the pick to break it up, which was the same for many feet deep. In this large gems were being found; it will doubtless be a very extensive mine. Near this, on Bell Fonta'ne, the adjoining farm, the hut was erected and plastered over with a mud mortar made of the light sandy surface soil, about the time or shortly after diamonds were discovered in south Africa, and when the mud became dry the hut was found literally studded with diamonds and was torn down, and about ninety taken out of the mortar, all very small and the whole of little value, and this is the house out of which the story originated that the houses built with the earth, were found studded with diamonds.

At the close of this chapter will be given the reported finds among the miners for upwards of a month.

As to the extent of the country where diamonds are now found and are likely to be obtained in South Africa, at present mines are being worked nearly or quite one

5 *

hundred miles up and down in the direction of the
course of the Vaal river, and on a belt, say fifty miles
wide ; that may enable the reader to form some idea of
the present range of the digging. But it must not be
supposed for a moment that the whole of this country
named is being worked, or ever will be, for the purpose
of diamond hunting. It includes all the copays and fields
heretofore mentioned, and they are only little spots in
it, and I think I can safely say that ninety hundredths
of the land, within the limits mentioned, will never be
touched with the view of diamond seeking; and if I
wished to be more exact, I should say ninety-nine hundredths would never be worked for that purpose. Nevertheless, these gems may hereafter be found in this region over a much wider range of territory than I have
mentioned and probably will be.

New places are being constantly discovered. Every
individual that owns or has possession of any land
near the fields is trying to convince himself and others
that it contains diamonds, for the soil chiefly is good for
nothing for agriculture, and, if found to be diamondiferous, may be of some value, and great efforts are made
by the interested parties to make people believe their
fields contain a mine of the precious gems; and to de-
monstrate the propositions sometimes made, the process
of inserting a few diamonds in the earth and finding
them again, just for the pleasure of it, no doubt, is gone
through with, remembering always to make a great
hurrah and disturbance about the finding, and, like Mrs.
Piffit, put it in the papers, constantly forgetting to mention how the diamond came to be found, which in this

case, like all men's works and unlike Nature's could be
easily explained. It may be too severe to assert this
as a positive fact; yet I am satisfied it has been done,
not only in one instance, but in several instances. What
motive could have induced any one to practice such deception, the reader may determine; it might have been
simply for the pleasure of being thought successful, or
for the purpose of leading others to try ground honestly
thought to contain diamonds, and to develope a place
where the individual alone had not the means of bringing it out ; or it might have been to set in motion any
other branch of trade or business connected with the
fields.

And I do not hesitate to say that while many fine
diamonds are obtained at the Vaal Fields, yet there is
almost any amount of deception, called humbugging,
practiced on and among the miners.

Notwithstanding to a limited extent prospecting is
honestly carried on by different persons, and new fields
are being opened even outside of the limits I have
named. As heretofore stated, when diamonds were first
discovered, the soil and nature of the country were but
little known by the white population, and as the territory
becomes better understood, and the first fields worked
out, new places will be sought for and found. Whether
the best places and richest diamond-producing soils are
now being worked, time only can determine, and wheth
er here or in any country diamond-seeking as a general rule is profitable, is very difficult to conclude. Some
one at the Vaal Fields started the report on some unknown hypothesis, perhaps taking the known finds,

that the actual profit of the miners as a whole was
not more than six pence per day; while another said he
would buy and give all the diamonds found for the
money spent by the miners in getting them, and a
handsome profit could be made in such a bargain.

But no one is able to judge correctly.   There is no
doubt that some who invest their money is this lottery
secure a rich prize, while others are only unfortunate
in their investment, and as the labor is carried on in
South Africa, it is considered a complete game of
chance.   I believe diamonds are worth the full price
set upon them, and those that are able to possess these
beautiful gems should not be scrupulous about their
cost, for they are procured chiefly in some wild, unsettled and otherwise unproductive land with many
hardships and deprivations, with great labor and expense, generally in a hot climate, under the burning
rays of a vertical sun; therefore, those whose circumstances enable them to wear these richest of ornaments
should have the heart to freely reward the patience
and labor required to bring such rich gems into their
caskets.   Their hearts should be like their jewels, the
richest and most precious of Nature's gifts.

The annexed is a list of the reported finds at the dates
specified, published in the *Diamond News*, a weekly
paper, printed at Pniel, South Africa, read by the author
while on the fields.   It should be stated that at many
of the diggings the paper had no correspondent, and
none of the finds at such places would be published, and
in the other localities only a list of those were given
which were generally known.   Many would be found

and only known by immediate neighbors, if at all, and of course such would not be reported. In the *News* of March 18, 1871, "Finds reported since last issue:"

AT CAWOODS HOPE.

Name of Finders.	No. of Diamonds.	Carats.
Spaulding....	1	4
W. Cowie..........	1	2¼
V. Horen...........	1	18
Fisher........ .	2	7½
Name unknown.. .	1	15⅞

AT COLESBERG COPAY.

Name of Finders.	No. of Diamonds.	Carats.
Churley & D........	3	4⅞

AT HEBRON.

Name of Finders.	No. of Diamonds.	Carats.
Mr. Fick	1	27

AT PNIEL.

Name of Finders.	No. of Diamonds.	Carats.
HolIand & N.	4	8⅝
McIntyre...........	3	
Jardine.	2	
R. J. Hall	1	37½
Jakins	1	4
Joilie & Cole..... .	1	2⅜
Hopely...........	1	6

In the *News* of April 1, 1871 (the paper of the intervening week the writer did not keep, and has not the list. But the finds averaged about the same each week.) "Finds reported since our last issue."

AT PNIEL.

Name of Finders.	No. of Diamonds.	Carats.
Perseverance Co. ..	2	15
Fleg	2	2
Dr. Hall............	1	1⅛
Jakins	2	
Sinclair's Party	2	
Capt. McIntyre. ..	1	1¼

AT DU TOITS PAN.

Name of Finders.	No. of Diamonds.	Carats.
Stewart....	3	
W. Short.... ...	1	28
J. J. Van Nickerk..	1	50

AT HEBRON.

Name of Finders.	No. of Diamonds.	Carats.
Lerussone	2	3½
G. Venter..	1	4⅝
T. Nicol	2	6
Watts	1	2
Bowles & Dell......	1	1¼

AT COLESBERG COPAY.

Name of Finders.	No. of Diamonds.	Carats.
Churley & D........	3	7¼

AT VICTORIA.

Name of Finders.	No. of Diamonds.	Carats.
Spes Bona Co......	2	3¾

AT CAWOODS HOPE.

Name of Finders.	No. of Diamonds.	Carats.
Schreiner...	1	9¾

AT HEBRON.

Name of Finders.	No. of Diamonds.	Carats.
Cameron....	1	4
Forrester...........	2	2
Dickinson & D.....	1	3
Donaghue....	2	2¼
Gaorter..........	1	2⅜
Geo. Thorne.......	2	4
Lumsden...... ...	1	3⅝
F. S. Vater...	1	11¼
Morris...	1	5⅝

The Port Elizabeth *Telegraph* and Eastern Province *Standard*, published at Port Elizabeth, South Africa, in its issue of May 26, 1871, has the following: " Latest Finds reported at the Diamond Fields."

AT DU TOITS PAN.

Name of Finders.	No. of Diamonds.	Carats.	Name of Finders.	No. of Diamonds.	Carats.
Van Vrede	1	79	Strit	1	23¼
Bretts	1	53½	Grobler	1	15½
Swanpoel	1	25½	Zex	1	15½
Same	1	5	Arns	1	8½
Nemo	1	15	Carl Gooste	1	8½
David	1	9½	Eybus	1	9¼

AT DU TOITS PAN.

Name of Finders.	No. of Diamonds.	Carats.	Name of Finders.	No. of Diamonds.	Carats.
Jessop	1	6¼	Tainton	1	3 4
Careon	1	6	Hins	2	6½
Duvenage	1	6	Moost	1	3½
Croft	2	7	Van Graan	2	2
Van Wyke	1	5¾	Golden Lace	2	3
Mc Kay	1	5	Lawler	2	4
Doctor	1	5	La Grande	1	3
Nemo	5	10¼	Liner	2	6¾
Burton	1	5½	Shart	1	1
Cosgrove	2	10	Venter	1	1¾
J. T.	1	3½	Hoole	3	2
Nell (of G. T.)	2	10½	Gregor	1	1¼
Brant	1	2½	Prince	1	1½
Schultz	4	5	Wilson	2	3
Miller	1	3	Du Plessis	1	1
Holliday	3	3	Swanepoel	1	½
Van Grans	3	4	Kruger	2	2¾
Finloson Co	1	1	Rothschild	1	½

AT PNIEL.

Name of Finders.	No. of Diamonds.	Carats.
Waller	1	
C. Jones	1	2½
Clark & Cole	2	12
Spes Bona Co	6	15
Taller	1	
Griffith's Party	1	6
J. Webb's Party	2	13
Dr. Howard's Party	1	5⅞
Jardine	4	

AT GONG-GONG.

Name of Finders.	No. of Diamonds.	Carats.
Bean & Lawrence	1	6½
A. Moss & Co.	1	6
Unknown	5	40
Antony	1	7

AT HEBRON, from 1st to 9th of May.

Name of Finders.	No. of Diamonds.	Carats.
Muir....	1	1
Boogstroem..........	1	1¾
Constantia Co	3	18
Calvinia Co..........	1	1⅞
G. Venter...	1	1
Mrs. Attwell.........	2	6½
J. Venter.....	1	9½
J. Every	1	2
Blackbeard	1	3
Crouch & Co...	2	3¾
Names unknown ...	4	126⅝
Letherius Co.	1	10½
Holliday....	1	2½
Donaghue	3	5¾
Hinton & Co..... ...	3	9
Daly	1	5½
Kingsley & Co......	1	6⅞

AT HEBRON, from 1st to 9th of May.

Name of Finders.	No. of Diamonds.	Carats.
Derry................	3	10½
J. Lewis.........	2	16
Collins....	2	8½
Rickets	2	3¼
Dennis & Dickinson	2	3½
Halse..	2	3½
A. Buckley..........	2	3⅛
E. Solomon	3	6½
T. Kafir.............	1	3⅞
H. Murphy	1	2
G. Niekerk..........	1	1½
Margraaff...	1	2½
A. W. Le Roy ...	1	2
Van Grassouw.......	1	1½
E. Hamilton.........	1	8¼
Currie & Co.....	1	1
Dell & Bowles... ...	2	3

AT VOSTERS RUSH.

Name of Finders.	No. of Diamonds.	Carats.
Sampson & Co.....	1	12
James Gleeson.....	1	82½
Goodhater	1	2
T. Muller....	2	13

AT HEBRON, from May 9th to May 17th.

Name of Finders.	No. of Diamonds.	Carats.
Dickinson & Co....	5	12½
W. Els.... . ..	2	3¼
Tainton	4	12
Thorne....	8	10⅛
S. Keefers	2	6½
A. Kalb............	2	6¾
Cato	2	3½
W. Mott	1	3
Clinkscales.... .. .	1	2
A. Law............	4	8⅛

AT HEBRON, from May 9th to May 17th.

Name of Finders.	No. of Diamonds.	Carats.
E. Goods	4	8
D. Schultz	3	4⅛
Berrange.	1	2¼
Raper........	1	1⅝
T. Smith . .	1	8⅜
Winter.............	1	16⅛
Brown....	2	16⅜
D. Myres	1	1½
E. Dugging	1	3
Forlorn Hope Co...	1	½
C. Hamilton... ...	1	4½

AT SPENCE'S.

Name of Finders.	No. of Diamonds.	Carats.
T. Sweetman.......	3	16⅞
Jason	2	11¾
Bisset..............	2	30
Trallip	3	16

CHAPTER VI.

BEING ready to return to my country and home, yet desiring to see and study all I could of the laws, manners and customs of the people and the land of Africa, I determined to return by way of Port Elizabeth, Algoa Bay. Therefore, on the 7th day of April, I left Pniel for the seashore in a transport wagon drawn by sixteen oxen, the carrier promising to perform the journey in thirty days, or about that time, and to take me to Port Elizabeth for £3 sterling. We left Pniel at eight o'clock in the evening—the traveling with the oxen being mostly done in the night, on account of the heat of the sun during the day, and also because the cattle will feed better in the day than in the night. The carrier with whom I was to go to the Port had three wagons, drawn by fifty oxen. Having taken loads from the Bay to the fields, he was now returning. All the carrying business in South Africa is performed with oxen and wagons similar to his. The weight of his loads up were, I think, 31,000 pounds, or a little over five tons to each load. He took down part of the way loading of wool, 24,000 pounds, or about four tons to each wagon. The wagons are made very heavy and strong, and will carry immense loads with proper roads and ordinary care. The first hundred miles of this homeward journey, from Pneil to Philopolis, was

performed without any loading except passengers and
their luggage. The passengers were one Englishman,
the carrier's father-in-law and his two sons, a Scotch-
man, a young Africanda—that is, a person born in
Africa of European parents—and the writer.

Each wagon was conducted by two Caffirs, one to
load and the other to drive the oxen, all superintended
by the conductor or owner; and with such a caravan
we started, leaving the Vaal River, with its riches and
solitude, behind us, and looking forward to home,
friends and civilization once more, though very many
thousands of miles away, and hoping the day was certain
and not far distant, when familiar faces would greet us
in a land we love so much.

The country through which we passed, both in the
Orange Free State and after crossing the Orange River,
in the Colony, for upwards of three hundred miles, and
till within sixty or seventy miles of Grahamstown, bore
very much the same aspect, consisting of undulating
plains between ranges of lofty mountains, or sometimes
a single mountain, rising up, cone-like, very much like
a volcano which had long ceased to throw out its burning lava and smoke. The plains were occupied by
farmers, mostly Dutch, the farms usually consisting of
several thousand acres, over which their flocks of
sheep and goats were allowed to roam, followed by
herdsmen, flocks generally consisting of many thousands of these animals, the cultivated portion of the
land being only a garden containing a few acres, enclosed with a stone wall or fence made of the low
shrubs that grow over some parts of the fields, and

generally situated below their dams of water, so as to
be irrigated in dry weather. But very few of these
farms have any streams or springs on them, and the
water is obtained by building a high circular dam across
some channel in which it flows in the rainy season and
retaining it in the basin thus formed.

Some years, in seasons of drought, the farmers have
been compelled to drive their flocks hundreds of miles
to the Vaal or Orange rivers to keep them from dying
of thirst, and, notwithstanding such efforts to save them,
they have perished by thousands, many losing their
entire flocks.

The scarcity of water seems to be the great drawback
to the country. Surely that disadvantage and tho
swarms of locusts that here abound and threaten destruction to every growing herb or green thing they light
upon would discourage most men from seeking a home,
and from the pursuit of wealth, in this country ; but farmers the world over are an independent, contented, hardy
race of beings, and among their numerous virtues, on
most elastic is that they are able to adapt themselves
to all kinds of soil, climate, or government, and, as a
class, to thrive and be happy wherever nature is sufficiently generous to yield her increase, though by never so
great labor, toil, and patience.

On the eighth day of April the teams were out-spanned,
ten miles from Pniel, to await the conductor who had
remained behind to close up his business. After the
oxen were turned loose to graze over the fields, the
Caffirs gather together some dry brush, a fire is kindled,
the pots and kettles are taken from their various hooks

and fastenings about the wagon. Coffee is first made and drank, and a dinner placed over the fire to cook. Only one meal a day is provided while the wagons are on the road, but coffee is made any number of times, and always at every stopping place.

Dinner consists of meat and bread, sometimes with boiled pumpkins, which take the place of potatoes, and the appetite this mode of life stimulates, it is very palatable. But with one meal a day, and of the quantity provided by the owners of these ox wagons, the traveler is hardly satisfied, and I found my arrangement with the carrier to provide myself with food while journeying with him to be the most acceptable, and I was not only able to have three meals a day usually, but also to get almost all the luxuries the country through which we passed afforded, one of which I will hereafter more particularly mention.

On the first day, after partaking of the coffee cooked in my quart cup, and the refreshments obtained before leaving Pniel, about which little domestic affairs in such circumstances one takes so much delight, especially in arranging upon his little table and happily contemplating as he sits down on the grass or stones before it. We walked about over the hills and plains, not being yet out of the diamond country, and thinking, like some of the most lucky, possibly we might pick up a large fortune in one little stone.

A large portion of the surface of the ground is here covered with gravel or water-worn pebbles, very much like that from which the diamonds are obtained. Here, too, is wild game in great abundance, the springbok,

spansbok, pows and other wild birds, and the sportsman
traveling with the ox teams finds many opportunities to
enjoy the excitement of the chase.

At sunset the conductor coming up, the herdsman
was warned to bring in the cattle by the clapping of
the drivers' immense whip, whose ringing sound, like
the discharge of a heavy loaded rifle, can be heard far
over the fields.

Coffee was again prepared, the teams were separated
and inspanned, the scattered culinary utensils were
gathered up, and again we were on our way, moving
along over the winding road with slow and certain steps.
Passing Du Toits Pan on the 9th; the 12th, we arrived at and outspanned near Jacobsdoll, a small town in
the Free State, but recently built up, consisting of a
few houses, a store, inn, and bottle store, as it is here
called, being a softened name for whisky shop. At
this hamlet, the farmers, whose wants in Africa must be
few and easily supplied, can dispose of their wool and
procure therefor raiment and wine. The little village is
situated in the centre of a vast level tract of land, with
no fences or enclosures to protect the houses or yards,
and a few scattered buildings look like the people, as
though their neighbors and friends were few, and far
away in some unattainable country. On either side, for
very many miles, nothing can be seen but the wide desolate plain. So far as land would satisfy the requirements of a large city, it would be a good location, on
which to build a modern Babylon. London or New
York would here find ample room to extend their
boundaries as wide as the wildest dreamer might wish;

and with all this wealth of land there are only these few
miserable apologies for buildings, to speak of the industry and boasted greatness of man.

What a pity it is that some modern philanthropist,
out from among all the pride and power of the human
race, cannot people the waste places of the earth
and make the deserts bloom with roses, filling the air of
all lands with the sounds of industry, and perfuming it
with the fragrance of the blooming flowers. Surely
God has not reserved these things to himself! Why
waste so much time and strength in war and strife?
Why cover the fields with the caskets of souls sent to
the spirit world while yet so young in this? Why do so
many poor people waste their energies and lives cooped
up in crowded cities and thickly populated countries,
when such broad fields but await the touch of the
magic wand of labor and civilization to make pleasant
homes, and beautiful gardens? To what purpose is so
much time, money and talent wasted in political strife
and civil discord, while such large portions of the earth
have as yet no politics or civil institutions? These
are questions for enlightened nations to solve—questions that may be propounded to kings, potentates and
rulers, when they stand before the bar of justice at the
final judgment.

O! what a wide field for the exercise of philanthropy
. the surface of this little planet yet exhibits! Could we
but imagine all nations and people throughout the wide
world, bending every faculty to the utilizing and beautifying all the inhabitable parts of the globe; the civilized
teaching the uncivilized; wealth yielding to necessity;

power stooping to justice, and afflictions borne down
and controlled by mercy; what an Eden might be made !
The earth stands with its wealth of soil, its beautiful
hills and plains, mountains and valleys, its groves and
forests covered with verdure—everything, and more
than when the innocent pair walked among the rich
foliage and flowers of their garden without toil; it now
but needs the sweating brow and strong hand to cut
away the thorns and thistles, and to plant trees and
flowers, and the earth will send forth her richest gifts.
Why should not nations turn their attention more to
these things ? The human mind must be employed, and
if directed into the channels of peace and industry—to
such an object as settling and beautifying all lands as a
garden—wars and strife must cease and yield to a
nobler ambition.

Leaving Jacobsdoll and the thoughts its scenery sug·
gested, we proceeded on our journey. But the reader
need not suppose I became so enthusiastic as to forget to
secure a new supply of provisions, which cannot at all
times be obtained on the road, especially where houses
and farms are several days' journey apart. The next
day after leaving this little embryo city, the teams were
out-spanned at one o'clock P.M., on the west bank of
the Riet river, after the stream had been forded, and
all the passengers and men went down to bathe in the
muddy water. None of the flowing streams I saw in
Africa were clear, all having the muddy appearance of
swollen rivers ; yet the dusty, tired traveller seeks their
refreshing waters in this hot, dry country, as it were
with natural instinct, and whenever an opportunity oc-

curs, to plunge into their cooling embaces ; it is improved with eagerness, after which one feels as fresh and new
as possible. And the waters of the Vaal river, though
always having the appearance of being thickly mixed
with a yellowish, red sand, yet I never bathed in any
water in any other country with such animating effects
as were received in this stream ; and even after their
hard day's work, perspiring much beneath the burning
sun, the miners generally, in the cool of the evening,
would bathe in this river without any bad effect.

This day, after leaving Jacobsdoil, for the first time
in my life I saw the locusts of Africa. Early in the
morning, as soon as the sun had fully risen above the
distant hills, looking towards the east we saw a dark
cloud winding about one of the mountain tops, spreading out and approaching the track in which our wagons
were going. Looking at them from that distance away,
they presented much the same aspect as a watery cloud
out of which rain would be expected. Flying with the
wind they soon began to fill the air over our heads, and
in fact all about us, dropping on the ground, and in
some places completely covering it with their bodies.
But the greater portion seemed to be continuing their
flight, and all the forenoon, during which we travelled
upwards of eight miles, the air over us was filled with
locusts, some flying high up and others so low we
could knock them down, or catch them with our hats as
they flew by directly overhead, looking like a thick heavy
snow-storm in a mild winter's day in the North. They
are very nearly of the form of the large-winged grass-
hopper of America, being much larger, and, besides

their brown wings or greenish; they have under those
a white gauze wing, which is wider than the dark
ones, and when flying overhead, reminds one of
large falling snow-flakes. The locusts are the
great pests of the country; if they alight on the
farmer's grain or gardens, everything green is swept
away as with a breath of wind; wherever they
settle down, if but for a few hours, when they again
rise, nothing is left on the spot where they rested
except the bare earth or leafless shrubbery; the cloth-
ing of the place seems to have been taken off, and left
like a dead, naked body. There is a kind of bird that
destroys the locusts, called locust-eaters. I think
they are obtained from the island of Mauritius. Some
person in South Africa is now importing them as an
experiment, to try if this enemy of the country could
be subdued. After the first, we saw swarms of these
insects a number of times while on our way to the sea.

It was about this time also (I think at the farm
where the teams were outspanned, the 15th of April),
as though all the ills of Africa were to be crowded on
my notice in one mass, that a Dutch farmer sold me for
food part of a sheep that died a natural death of some
disease. This was one of the luxuries I promised, in a
former page, to mention. When a lung disease or something of that kind prevails among their flocks, and the
sheep die of it, the Dutch dress, cook, and eat them;
and I suppose the man who sold me the flesh was innocent enough in his heart, or, if he reflected at all
about it, he probably thought, being among the Dutch,
I must do as the Dutch do.

But if such food is palatable to them, I must say that
I think when a stranger among them is interested in a
case in which life or death is in question, he ought to
be allowed to exercise a choice as to whether the death
shall be natural or artificial, especially under the laws
of hospitality; and this man ought to have had the
frankness to say the sheep not only died, but died of
sickness naturally; then I would have reciprocated his
generosity, and allowed him to give his article of barter
all the other recommendations he saw fit to bestow,
and it could have been purchased or not; one being
controlled, doubtless, by the degree of starvation he
was enduring. But I was not imposed upon in this
way the second time. The difference in the appearance
of the meat can readily be distinguished, the blood remaining in the flesh of those that die of disease. And,
although as we passed along calling at the outspanning
farms, I saw many pieces of the same kind hanging up
in their kitchens, from which apparently the cooks were
carving the families' daily food, yet I never again desired to try this luxury, and, thank God, I was not compelled to.

On the 17th of April we arrived at Philopolis, another
small town in the Orange Free States, and about one
hundred miles from Pniel. Here we remained two days,
and the wagons were partially loaded with wool. Phil·
opolis has only one principal street; but some very
pretty residences, with shade trees, arbors and gardens.
The business, like that of the other towns, consists
simply of receiving from the farmers their wool and
hides, and furnishing them with the few necessaries,

6

they require.   The Dutch have built here a very fine
church, and adorned its tower with a clock, the tones
of which, as its hammer struck the hour of day,
called up pleasant memories, and led us to believe
we were again coming back into the world.

There is also an English church in this village.   The
Dutch of South Africa are strong in their religious faith,
and their fidelity seems to have called forth a generous
rule of conduct in the erection of their churches.   In
Colesberg and Craddock they have fine church buildings, both as to stability and beauty of architecture, especially in Craddock, which boasts that it has the finest
church in the Colony, and it certainly far exceeds the
expectations of the stranger.   No one would think of
finding in so small a village, and in a country so thinly
populated, such a richly constructed church.   It is built
of finely cut dark gray granite, in the Corinthian style
of architecture, with a high broad porch, the roof of
which is sustained by Corinthian pillars of the same
cut stone.

It stands in the centre of the town on a square plot
of ground, enclosed with a fine fence, on a stone base,
all to correspond with the building.   The building is said
to have cost thirty thousand pounds sterling.   It is a
fine and endurable specimen of church architecture, and
the spirit of the people that conceived and carried out
such an enterprise in this land is worthy of imitation
by Christian worshippers in any country in the world.

Leaving Philopolis on the 19th day of April, our
roads for some distance lay through a more mountainous district, with more variable scenery, sometimes

winding round wild and romantic cliffs or in rocky gorges, and again coming out on a lovely landscape with a farmer's cottage nestling close to the base of the hills, covered with his flocks, presenting a scene of rural beauty and striking contrasts, such as delight the painter's eye.

On the 20th, at noon, the wagons arrived at and crossed the Orange river on a "punt." This is the boundary line between the Colony and the Free State.

A large share of the carrying trade from Port Elizabeth to the interior is done over the same road we were now travelling, and at this time of the year the heavily laden wagons were frequently passing. The Orange river flows between high sandy banks at the point where I crossed it, both in going and returning from the Diamond Fields, and at either place several wagons were waiting their turns to be taken across; but in going up the passenger wagon had the preference, and we were not then delayed. But here the teams had to take their turn, after those which had previously arrived at the banks had been ferried across. The labor of drawing the great loads up the banks after crossing the river is very exciting to one unaccustomed to witnessing such work; but the ignorance and cruelty of the drivers takes away much of the pleasure of the occasion. When the punt touches the landing, two span of the oxen, consisting of sixteen or eighteen pairs or yokes forming a long team, are attached to the wagon, and amid the crashing of the immense whips and the yelling and screeching of the natives, they are started up the ascent, the wide wheels plowing deep into the sand,

sometimes sticking fast with the weight, like a great
moving house.   Then woe to the poor oxen if they do
not draw it on the second or third trial ; some of them
will get a cruel cutting up with the long whips, (or a
"sham buck,") the stinging lash of which they cannot
escape—the large number holding each in its place in
the line ; sometimes the yoke has worn away the skin
on their necks and shoulders, and yet they are compelled
to draw against the bare flesh.

The next day after crossing the Orange the teams
were outspanned at the village of Colesberg, and tho
balance of the loading procured in wool and hides.
This town is quite a pleasant little place of six or seven
hundred white inhabitants, a number of churches,—
among which the largest, the Dutch Presbyterian, not
yet completed, is to be very costly and extensive—a
court house, and also uniformed police force, of course
small ; I think I saw two or three of these officers pa-
trolling the streets.   The village also has its reservoir
of water and fountains supplied by some spring or
stream from the mountains, which rise on either side to
the height of hundreds of feet.   At Colesberg the people were complaining of the dullness caused by so many
having left it and the neighborhood and their business to
go to the Diamond Fields.   But nearly every one of the
towns in Africa, except Port Elizabeth, through which
we passed, presented the same appearance of desertion
and stupidity.   Whether they were always so, or it is
caused by a lack of interest and declining trade, I cannot say.

From Colesberg, the road for a number of days lay

through a country of plains and mountains, like that
which I have attempted to describe on former pages ;
and our life while passing over it was unvaried from
the usual routine of out-spanning, in-spanning, cooking,
eating, walking, sleeping, losing the oxen while grazing,
and the next day or two finding them again, and taking
all the pleasure we could, as time wore away and our
journey of life as well as of distance was drawing nearer
its end, sometimes doubting which would close first.

On the night of the 20th of April, one of the dessle-
booms was broken while passing through a rough muddy
place. This is a frequent occurrence with these heavy
loads, and extra poles are commonly carried, but there
being none for this occasion, all the teams must come
to a halt for a day or two, till the place of the broken
shaft could be supplied from the neighboring farm, ten
miles away. The break down occurred about midnight,
and of course nothing could be done till morning, (so
the carrier thought). As the teams had been nearly a
week going fifty miles, and becoming weary and dis-
couraged with the continual delays, also being quite out
of provisions, I determined to proceed a day's march on
foot ; therefore, as soon as the gray dawn gave any signs
of the coming day, taking up my blanket and pilgrim's
staff, I proceeded on over the lonely road for ten miles
before coming to any habitation, which, under ordinary
circumstances, would be considered a long walk in the
morning, before breakfast, and would be deemed longer
still if it was known the meal, at its conclusion, was to
be made of sea biscuit and sardines, which was all I
could then get at a winkle by the way. But a good

appetite is easily satisfied, and sitting down near a little creek that run through the farmer's garden, I took as much comfort and pleasure in my frugal repast as ever a profusely loaded table could afford, in a country where everything was plentifully supplied.

After breakfast, spreading out my blanket on the dry ground, I lay down upon it; the heat from the warm rays of the meridian sun being fanned away by a cool breeze that blew over the heath, the wearied limbs relaxed, the eyelids closed, and sweet slumber drove away all dreams of lands or labors, and for a few hours I was in that state as to the world that we all will be when we have gone to sleep, never to wake again on mortal cares or troubles, except the current of life still flowed in its channels with the power to quickly rouse the slumbering senses. After a refreshing siesta, I again took up my blanket and trudged along till four o'clock P. M., when I arrived at an inn and farm called Wilder Beast Flats, where I could stay till the wagons came up.

The loquacious landlord of this place, who formerly had been, as he affirmed, an English school teacher, was very much afflicted with a diamond mania, and because he found a few smooth pebbles on the surface of his land, had wrought himself up to the pitch of believing that diamonds could there be found, but he had not the means (or was too indolent) to prospect, and like Micawber and many more of the human race, was waiting for something to turn up, or for things to develope themselves. I remained at this inn two days, during which there was an auction sale of sheep, stock and im-

plements of husbandry on an adjoining farm, which I
attended.

The farmer was selling all his effects for the purpose
of removing to the diamond diggings. It may interest
the reader to know the value of farm stock in this country; there was a good attendance of buyers, and doubtless the property was sold for its full market value.
Between two and three thousand sheep and several hundred Angora goats and some common goats were sold.
The poorest flock of sheep were sold for 4s. 6d. each,
the best brought 7s. 0d., the Angora goats were
sold some for 13s. 0d., and some for 17s. 6d. The
bucks were imported and were not sold, though upwards
of £30 were offered, many of them when imported
costing £100.

The wagons coming on the third day, I joined them
again and we proceeded on the road. On the night of
the 29th of April, we crossed the beds of Big Fish and
Brack rivers, which are but a few rods apart. There
was scarcely any water in either. Like many of the
rivers in Africa, in the wet season, when at times the
rain pours down in torrents, the high banks will become
filled with a rapidly flowing stream; but when the rain
is over, the hot sun soon dries up the sources of supply,
and within a very short period of time the large rivers
become but empty channels.

On the second day of May, passing through Craddock,
the teams were outspanned early in the morning a little
way from the town, giving us a full day to look about
the place. I do not think much more can be said about
this village than has already been written—it is the

largest town we had yet come to since leaving the
"Fields," still it is small; but there seems to be an air
of neatness and quiet pleasantness about the little ham-
lets that would make a residence there for one seeking
retirement for a few months or years from the cares and
troubles of a busy city life really charming.

The following day after leaving Craddock we came
to a halt under the shadow of a mountain, near the base
of which the Big Fish river ran. The mountain was
one of those of volcanic appearance heretofore mentioned, looking from the plain below it as though in past
years its top had been the smoking crater of an active
volcano. It being upwards of two thousand feet high, I
thought it was a good opportunity to look from its top
on the country around—to "view the landscape o'er."
The ascent was very steep, and would have been difficult and dangerous but for the brush and shrubbery that
covered its sides, to which I could cling and pull myself
up. Reaching the top and stepping out on a projecting
cliff I found the toil and labor of the ascent all repaid
with the view before me. There was to be seen from the
great height another one of the most extensive and beautiful landscapes, and such as men very seldom behold,
the channel of the narrow river, bordered on either bank
with the willow, fir, and thorn trees, winding and turning in many different ways, followed closely with its
little border of green foliage through the whole vast
plain, appearing to issue out of a mountain range several days' journey northward, taking its zig-zag course,
passing at the foot of the elevation on which I stood,
on, on, and on, losing itself in the distant mountains

towards the south. Back of my position, was continued the range of the one I had climbed, rising still higher, and its sides looking back to the right or left covered with verdure, on which, far in the distance, up its sloping sides, the cattle of the teams were grazing. Before me, on either hand, was a great plain very slightly undulating, with here a green spot and there a yellow, or the shade of dried stems of grass, now a bare red soil lending its hue, and then a grey clay, varying the scene almost every shade the earth, the shrubs, the withered grass, or green herbage could give, with an occasional white farm-house and garden dotting the picture. Directly below were collected numerous wool-loaded wagons, and with the men about them looking like little children. In the horizon the plain disappeared and the tops of the mountains intercepted the sky all around. Indeed, it was a picture whose equal is seldom witnessed, and never by but few; and if ever a person feels like praising "the Lord for his goodness, and for his wonderful works to the children of men," it is when standing on some eminence like this, for the first time, and drinking in, at one sweep of the vision, so much of the creation of His hands. Man may paint a pleasing picture on canvas and exhibit the varied colorings of art; he can trace mountains, hills, plains, and valleys, the rising or setting sun tinging the clouds with its blended rays, the grazing flocks and herds, and the cottage, with its lawns and groves, and all the scenes of nature, while, at the same time, in comparison with the canvas God spreads before us, he but paints his weakness, and proves how frail are all his powers.

G *

It would seem that if each of the human family, alone, could stand one hour in the solitude of nature, surrounded on every side with the awful works of creation, with their beauty and their greatness, and in earnest thought contemplate the mighty whole, every one must fall down and worship that Being whose will could establish even what he sees and knows, much more the lands and seas and worlds, the suns and stars he can never view. As the setting sun was sinking below the tops of the distant hills, I took up my staff, and with sober (if I express my true feelings, I may say melancholy) thoughts descended to the wagons with new feelings, and impressions that cannot be obliterated from the mind before that hour when sense and feeling fail.

Again we travelled on several days, stopping a day now and then to look for lost oxen, and once breaking another dessleboom, till the ninth day of May, and to within sixty miles of Graham's Town, when in the early part of the evening the teams had just got fairly under way and down went one of the fore wheels of our wagon, with every spoke and felloe destroyed with one crash.   And here was another delay of two days at least, for a new wheel must be sought and made at a village several miles away, and brought and put in the place of the broken one, before the wagons could go on.   Begining to think we never should get to the Bay, the thirty days in which the carrier had promised to perform the journey being already past, and yet we were one hundred and fifty miles, or one third of the distance unaccomplished, and I began to look about for a swifter conveyance.   Fortunately a four-horse passenger cart,

which had passed us during the day, was stopping at a
roadside inn but a short way ahead, and was to proceed
to Graham's Town at once, so I thought, as they write
in novels, rescue was at hand in the last moments of
despair, or, as my case was not quite so desperate, for I
had enjoyed the life, things appeared to turn up about
as I wished to have them, and believing duty was now
urging me to hasten on, I bid farewell to my home, not
"on the sea" but on the ox wagon, and arrived in Graham's Town the next day at noon.

Graham's Town is a very pleasant city, lying in a
hollow, surrounded by high hills, and here the soil
appeared to be more productive, and the fields were covered with their mantle of green verdure. But the town
itself presented that same aspect of listless monotony
and decay of all the other interior villages, and which
never could have given the place its present magnitude
and beauty. I saw, too, in passing through the streets,
many of its large stores and warehouses were empty
and closed, and learned that real estate was very low in
value. It did seem too bad that with such a fine climate
and so much natural beauty so many pleasant homes
must be closed and deserted for want of resources to
maintain them. One cannot but carry away, after visiting the interior of Cape Colony, the impression that the
business of the towns is decreasing; that there is no
spirit of modern enterprise among the Dutch people
beyond securing the necessaries or perhaps comforts of
life; no advancement from the ways of their fathers.
And the English residents, in general, are only in the
country temporarily, to make all the money they can as

soon as possible, and with it to return to their native land, and have no thoughts of making this sunny clime their home, or of bringing forth its resources beyond the scope in which immediate and profitable returns would be expected. But to hasten on. During the week in which I arrived in Graham's Town I obtained a conveyance to Port Elizabeth. On the 13th day of May, while yet some thirty miles from the Port, when passing over the high-lands, the ocean came in view, and we could hear the roar of its beating surf. It was a cheering sight to me to gaze once more out on the blue expanse of its boundless waters, for I could look over the rolling waves and reflect that my friends, and family, and home were on the other side, and I longed again to embrace the loved ones whom I believed there awaited me, and to mix with the busy world of life and activity in my own country. On the 15th I arrived in Port Elizabeth, and my travels in Africa were concluded.

CHAPTER VII.

WITHOUT any notice of my passage home and the many days on the sea, made pleasant by the little party of passengers and the kind-hearted, social captain, I should deem my book quite incomplete; for socially it was the most agreeable period of my absence : besides, there were many little incidents took place aboard the "Alma," which, if the reader had been with us far out on the "great deep," with so much solitude around, would, no doubt, have interested him ; and if the relation fails to make the occurrences attractive, it must, I suppose, be laid to the feeble powers of my pen. But, dear reader, if you have had the patience to peruse these pages thus far, and have found any pleasure or profit in following, in your imagination, the outlines of my journey, and the pictures of nature I have endeavored to portray, you will certainly bear with me a few moments longer while I perform a task no less pleasing than easy of accomplishment.

If I have written up to this page to enable the reader to spend an hour in thought among the scenes of a country visited by but few, and whose "sunny clime" is but little known, I desire now to pen a few lines at the beginning of this concluding paragraph, to gratify my own active sense of duty, and to render to one of a class of men who, as a rule, receive too little of the

world's gratitude, that praise and commendation he so
justly merits.   That one was Captain O. Christensen, of
the Norwegian barque "Alma," of Tonsberg, with whom
I obtained a passage from Algoa Bay to New York.
If any man has a generous heart, he has ; if any man
treads the deck of a fast-sailing ship, he does ; if any
one commands an obedient, cheerful, hearty crew, it is
he.   The barque was loaded with wool, bound to the
port of New York: there were aboard as passengers,
Mrs. Christensen, the wife of the captain, Captain and
Mrs. Doane of Boston, and the writer.

On Saturday, the 27th day of May, being informed
the vessel was ready to sail and only awaited a favora-
ble breeze, the captain's boat took me on board, amidst
a heavy swelling sea rolling into the harbor, with a gale
of wind blowing from the south-east.   On the next
morning, the wind having veered round, and the pilot
being at hand, the anchor was hoisted, the sails set, and
the "Alma" glided beautifully and quickly out from
among the shipping and the dangerous harbor of Port
Elizabeth.

The pilot descending to his boat, with his crew rowed
round to the windward, gave us three parting cheers, to
which we heartily responded, and the ship was soon
again alone far out on the deep blue waters, her prow
cutting the waves, scattering the spray abroad as she
dashed along over the main.   On the morning of the
third day out, two full-rigged ships were sighted far a-
head, taking the same course as the "Alma," which
passed them during the day, and although they were
carrying all sail when the sun had set, only the tops of

their spars were visible in the distant horizon astern of the vessel on which we rode. Near the island of St. Helena two other ships were overtaken and passed; and before crossing the Equator we had passed two others that had left that island considerably in advance of us, and, in fact, all the ships seen on the same course as the barque were passed by her; for which reason I believed myself justified in asserting that Captain Christensen treads the decks of a fast-sailing vessel.

I will not weary the patience of the indulgent reader in detailing the many little incidents of a pleasing and social nature occurring on the vessel during her passage; everything that could be done to dispel the lingering hours and drive away care was cheerfully permitted; and the sailors, though there was free intercourse between the officers and men, were most industrious, polite and obedient to every order.

The 23d of June was celebrated by them as a holiday, "Midsummer," it being the custom in Norway. In the evening a bonfire was suspended from the fore-yard arm, by the light of which the jolly tars sent forth their joyous huzzas, with marching and music.

The 4th of July, Captain Doane and his wife being Americans, we kept Independence day with proper festivities as may be fully believed. Is it strange that far from home and friends and native lands, in the midst of the great deep, many, very many leagues from that fertile earth on which all one's hopes of life depend, and even in the tropical latitudes under the vertical rays of the burning sun near the Equator, with the deep, fathomless sea on every side extending its restless waves many times beyond the power of vision, we should remember those days of joy and festivity so often kept in safety near our own fireside? No! it is not wonderful; it is rather an evidence of the advancement of men, not only out of the darkness of dread and superstition, but also in the knowledge of the seas, and in skill to navigate swiftly over all its waves, and ride from land to land with confidence and safety, using the elements of nature, appreciating the goodness of that Omniscient Being who made all things, and gave man the power and skill above all mortal creatures, making even the elements, the earth, air, and sea, subservient to his happiness.

On the 4th day of July, in 6° north latitude, 30° west longitude, quite a fishing expedition was commenced. Captain Doane took the spear from its place, and with a line attached to it, holding it in his hand, stepped peacefully out on the chains under the jib-boom, and thrust it delicately down into a beautiful little fish that was laughing in the water near the prow of the ship. But the spearman had sent spear-rope and all after the dear little creature, and part of the line remaining on deck Captain Christensen and I had the joy of catching the fish, which was done by lifting it out of the sea on board as gently as possible. The poor, distressed, shipwrecked swimmer proved to be a veneta, or species of small dolphin, which had received the barbed iron in its back very close to the head, and you may believe humanity caused us to relieve it of its painful effects as quickly as we could with proper surgical skill. Others were likewise taken in · a similar

manner afterwards; but the grand haul took place the
next day but one, July 6th, and also the day after that.
On the 6th, about half-past nine A.M., a shark was seen
playing round some object in the sea near the side of
the ship. The captain thought best to let the sailors
take him aboard, remarking that he liked to catch them
because they were dangerous to a person who might
happen to get into the sea, as they had been known to
take a human leg or arm for their dinner many a time,
and on deck they could be better managed than in
their native home. Therefore, a large hook was got out,
attached to a strong rope, and baited with a piece of
salt meat, when it was thrown out towards his canni-
balship in the water. The shark, unlike most all pisca-
tory animals, instead of becoming alarmed and
swimming away from the splashing of the hook in the
sea, started at once towards it, the sailors throwing it
with as much noise as possible, the fish, doubtless, being
taught by instinct that where there is a splash near a
ship there must be food that he desired, and he was one
of a kind that never thinks of danger. He came near,
and at once made at and took the bait and hook into
his mouth, and as suddenly the sailors hove away at the
line ; no doubt the shark soon decided he had taken a
larger mouthful than was compatible with digestion ; at
least, I was led to believe it had arrived at that conclusion from the great effort made to get rid of it, for he
lashed the water, and darted here and there with so
much force, that for some time it was difficult for two
men with their strongest powers of muscular persuasion
to bring him to their terms of compromise even, which

contained no other condition than that he should come
on deck, after which the sailors were so lenient they
promised to hold a consultation as to what disposition
should afterwards be made of him, and the terms of
peace to be granted, and the treaty with fish to be allowed. Two or three other men, putting in their arguments about this time on the side of the sailors, and his
sharkship seeing he was alone in opposition, finally
consented to yield the point, after which, like the fear-
less and powerful creature he was, he acknowledged the
superior strength of the lords of creation, when, directed
by combined wisdom and skill, and to heighten the glory
of the achievements of his conquerors, he grandly displayed his expiring strength before them.

   After the shark had been lifted on deck it was decided, in a council of war held by his captors, that no
reliance could be placed on a treaty made with another
species of beings; besides, it did not appear that this
one was invested with any powers from his race, as
plenipotentiary or envoy extraordinary, to make an
alliance with man ; and not being able to give any rea-
sonable account for his presence, it was determined that
he was a relentless enemy taken while on an expedition
of destruction of some human being, and in order to
prevent the danger of further loss of life from his unpit-
ying vengeance he must die. He was executed accord-
dingly. It was said by those who had seen others,
that this one was small. It measured seven feet in
length, and would weigh, I should judge, fully one hundred pounds ; its color was dark on the back, with a
lighter shade on the belly, with a smooth skin, a large

broad mouth nearly under the centre of its head ; the
two fore-fins were nearly a foot in length, broad and
strong.   Its death was effected by cutting off the tail,
when the blood streamed out of an artery near the centre of the back bone ; the tail was two feet long, and
very wide.   The back-bone was taken out as it would
make a beautiful walking-stick; the liver was also saved
for the oil it contained, after which the balance was
thrown again into the sea.

I will relate one more successful catch which took
place the next day, just before sunset. The captain then
discovered a shoal of porpoises playing in the sea just
before the prow of the vessel.   This time a harpoon
was ordered out, and as soon as it could be got ready,
the carpenter stepped out under the jib-boom and at once
sent the spear home into the side of one of them, which
was just then passing beneath him.   All hands at once
began to haul away at the line, but as the porpoise came
out of the water, it was seen that the harpoon having
entered the side low down and into the entrails, it had
not a sure hold, one of the barbs being already quite
out of the fish, and the other only holding in the skin.
The order was given to get hold of its tail as quick as
possible, and as it was drawn up to the rail of the ship,
the two captains got him by that handle, Captain Doane
crying out get a bow-line, which I tried to do by jumping about, not knowing what a bow line was but afterwards found it to be nothing more or less than a
rope, which was quickly fastened around the tail of the
porpoise just as the harpoon came wholly out; so it was
brought in by the rope over the rail, while the ladies

were clapping their hands at the success of the enterprise.

The porpoise was a beautiful fish to look at, without any qualification. It was six feet long and would probably weigh upwards of seventy-five pounds; its color was dark blue, darker than the blue sea, or the sky, throughout its whole body, and its skin bore a smooth polish resembling dark, blue glass; its head and jaws run out to a small point, between one and two inches in diameter at the tip, and well proportioned, with neatly curved lines in the mouth, filled with beautiful rows of pointed teeth, upwards of eighty on each jaw, both above and below. Its skin, while wet from the sea, shone like a mirror, its shape was perfect and faultless. It was the most beautiful fish I had ever seen, and I doubt whether there are any that exceed it in perfect form, proportions and color.

After getting it on deck, it was stuck with a knife, as is the custom in slaughtering hogs, and it died much like one of those animals. Its body and blood were warm, which I am informed is never the case with any other kind of fish. The porpoise is said to be very good for the table when properly prepared, but the flesh is dark colored. The liver fried in butter was placed on our table the next morning, and it was excellent, and could not be distinguished, by taste, from pig's liver; there was no fish taste to it whatever. The fins were saved as curiosities; the lower jaw was taken off for the oil it contained, being very valuable, and is used by jewelers in oiling clocks and watches. The balance was given up to the sea.

Thus we had enjoyed quite a glorious time at fishing; and one who appreciates such sport must conclude that it furnished great pleasure and satisfaction to have such opportunities of passing away the time. The ladies, too, enjoyed the sport, if we are to judge by the interest exhibited in the expressive face, and their presence added zest to our pleasure and heightened the delicacy of our operations.

Another, and not the least among the many sources of pleasure on board the "Alma," was that of music. Music! What feelings even the utterance of those two syllables awaken. It is the sweetest sounding word and the most significant in the English language. 'Tis music to my ear! In what breast does it not call up joys long since buried beneath the weight of years? Whose bosom does not swell with emotions of pleasure at the notes of the soft-toned instrument, or the warbling accents of the human voice? Where beats the heart that has not throbbed at the melody of some voice that has since passed away, and is only to be treasured in memory's dreams? In the halls of mirth, music adds its charms; within the sacred limits of the family hearth-stone, it sheds its soothing influence; before the battle, it rouses the soul to deeds of noble daring; it thrills the orator, and lifts up his swiftly flowing thoughts; it cheers the mariner on his lonely way; it carries a sacred influence within the walls of the consecrated temple of the Most High, and its requiem is the last pleading act of love over the grave of the departed spirits that have winged their flight to the regions of endless praise, where the music of the spheres swells

the anthems and wafts the loud hosannahs in that ce-
lestial choir, whose theme is God, and whose song is
without end! Music is nature's charm. The birds in
spring usher in the balmy air of the morning of the
year. The robin carols his notes at the rising of the
sun over the distant budding groves ; and the branches
of the forest trees ring with the music of the feathered
songsters as the opening leaves clothe them anew in
their foliage. The heath, the meadow and orchard are
filled with the sounds of unfolding nature, as the gentle
wind disturbs the flowers of the blossoming fruit or bends
the young blades of the waving grass, to raise the harmony
of its Æolian harp. The bleating of the flocks, the low-
ing of the herds upon the pasture land, the whistle of
the wood-chuck as it enters its den, and the chuckle of
the squirrel as it leaps from tree-top to tree-top, the
bubbling of the running brook, the heavy tones of the
river fall, the whirling of the wind through the thick
woods, and in autumn the falling leaves, all contribute
to swell the song of nature till it rings over hills and
through valleys, in the forests and on the plains, with
the music of its choral harmony vibrating the air round
the whole earth. Music was one of the happy events
on board the "Alma." The Swedish nightingale and
Swiss songsters are noted for their proficiency in this
pleasing art, and Norway will yet bring forth her mock-
ing bird, or her Lind, or Nilsson to charm the world.

One among the crew of the barque played the violin
with much skill; and the wife of the captain, who
sometimes assisted, accompanied the organ with her
voice in some beautiful songs, which in their native lan-

guage were exceedingly sweet, and could not fail to excite applause from the musical critic.

All I can wish, is, that if any tired spirit seeks rest and refreshment by a long voyage upon the sea, and is wafted on his way over the great deep only by the breezes that may arise to fill the white sails of his ship, he mey meet on his voyage with amusements as congenial to his taste, as I found while on my passage from Algoa Bay to my country and home. Our voyage was made with constant good weather, but with very light winds and many days of calm, except on Tuesday, the 25th day of July, while passing between the Island of Bermuda and America. In the morning of that day, soon after breakfast the ship was struck with a heavy gale of wind, accompanied by rain, with thunder and lightning; several of the sails, before they could be taken in, were shivered like brittle paper, and the tall masts bowed before the tempest as bended willows. It continued squally throughout the day, but in the evening the wind went down, and the sea, which had been rolling its waves mountains high, again became calm. The "Alma" continued on her course with very little wind, making slow progress. On the morning of the 31st day of July it became evident we were nearing port, from the number of ships and small sail about us. At about noon of this day a pilot came on board, and at four o'clock in the evening land became visible near Barnegat's Point. On the 1st day of August, passing along the shore, and with Long Branch in the distance and its immense hotels looming up from among the numberless cottages, with the green hills in the back-ground, we were once more in full view of the welcome shores of America.   At three o'clock P. M. a tow boat was secured, and a strong breeze springing up at the same time, our ship came into port very quickly, passing Fort Lafayette, the forts on Staten and Long Islands, with the land heavily clothed with verdure on every side.   As the vessel entered the harbor the wind died away, and the sun, which had been obscured by the thunder cloud, came out bright and beautiful, seemingly greeting us at the door of our native land and our home, and it rejoiced the heart, at least of one returning wanderer.

CHAPTER VIII.

IT has been my object thus far, as well as my inexperienced pen would permit, to set forth the facts coming under my observation, and some of the impressions I had received on the journey, and while in South Africa and at the Diamond Fields, leaving the reader to form his own judgment about the country and the mines.

If any one should think of visiting this part of the world for pleasure, or of emigrating there for the purpose of seeking their fortunes or increasing their wealth, to such I may say, in conclusion, that the sea voyage, especially in steamers by way of England, leaving America in October or November, calling at the various Islands between England and the Cape, is a very pleasant trip. The voyager becomes thoroughly accustomed to the sea; he leaves behind the biting frosts of winter, arriving in Cape Town in February, when the sun has again inclined to the north, and the hot weather there is past; spending two or three months in the country, and returning to arrive home in June. He will remain in South Africa in the midst of the harvest and fruit season, when vegetables are new and fresh, and oranges, peaches, pears, grapes, etc., are in great abundance, and the climate at this season is healthy and delightful.

Any person desiring to flee from the cares of busi-

7

ness for a few months, or seeking to renew their health
by travelling, will find, I believe, the time and money
spent in such a journey all that could be desired. Of
the hot season at the Cape, of course I cannot speak
from personal experience; it is doubtless more or less
accompanied with the sickness among the people to
which all hot countries and seasons are subject. Yet it
is said that South Africa is at all times particularly healthy.

When I left America I was thin in flesh, bilious, and,
from long and steady sedentary employment and the
cares of a business life, my constitution was generally
enfeebled. During the first part of the journey I grew
still poorer, suffering much from sea-sickness, eating
hardly sufficient food to support life, besides being afflicted with a severe cold. But before arriving at the
Cape of Good Hope I began to mend, and as soon as I
landed there, my appetite being excellent, and living on
the fruit and fresh vegetables the country then afforded,
I gained in health and strength very rapidly, and when
starting for home my fellow passengers out to Africa
flatteringly said they could scarcely believe I was the
same man, I had so much improved in appearance. And
I arrived home feeling renewed in health and vigor, prepared again to enter upon the duties of a laborious pro-
fession.

As to the Diamond Fields, they are very much of a
lottery, and, like any other speculation in which a fortune is sometimes quickly and easily made, there are
more blanks than prizes, and I do not believe money
invested there, as the digging is now carried on, as a

rule, is profitable, and I cannot encourage any person to go to the South African Diamond Fields with the anticipation of realizing sure success in seeking wealth, or even with the hope of obtaining a fair remuneration for his capital and labor. The chances are rather that he will lose all his costs and expenses. And when reading about Diamond Fields, and the finding of stones of great value, it must be remembered that in such accounts only the successful ones are spoken of. When a man is said to have found a diamond valued at £20,000 or $100,000 he is one among thousands. And then his gem must be sent home, and cut, and a purchaser found who is willing to expend such a large sum for one of these jewels, unless the finder is willing to take much less than a fair price; and the expense incurred in transporting, insuring, cutting and setting the prize reduces the value very much, besides taking much time.

There are many persons on the fields who have found diamonds valued at one, two, or even three thousand pounds sterling, which if they had sold them at once and taken the money and returned home, would have made a handsome profit. But they think they are not offered enough, and attempt to send them to Europe, and, getting a considerable sum advanced by the consignee, continue their labors, perhaps with greater expense and outlay, and when the return of the sale arrives to their hands they find it nearly used up from commissions, expenses, and their own extravagance. Again, I know one of a party of four who found a gem for which they were offered £6,000 on the spot, but deeming it too little, sent it to England, where only £3,-

000 would be offered for it, consequently they were having it cut and sent to India, and during the time the party were spending all the advances they could obtain in idleness and dissipation at Port Elizabeth, and it appears as though the harvest of the successful miners, as a general thing, turns out in about the same way—fully complying with the maxim that "money easily got is more easily spent."

If a person has from one to three thousand dollars they can spare without detriment to themselves or those dependent on them, and with it desires to try his luck in the lottery of the Diamond Fields of South Africa, then I have no objection; there is a chance of reaping a golden harvest, but at the same time there are a thousand chances that all the money will be spent, getting in return, perhaps, only experience and wisdom. which, it is said, is better than rubies. No one can give the mines a fair trial with less than £200 in his pocket when he has arrived at them; and, if unsuccessful, he wants means sufficient to pay expenses home. With such a sum one can buy his implements, hire three or four men, natives, and with them work in the fields six months, which I would consider a fair trial of the business. The current money used throughout South Africa is the English sterling, pounds, shillings, and pence, and, for that reason, in speaking of prices and expenses, I have used that denomination.

The cost of living at the Diamond Fields is not dear, board being from fifteen shillings upwards per week; all the necessaries are as cheap as in any country. But persons going there without means do not find it like gold hunting, where, as a rule, industry will find means to cover expenses.

At diamond digging many have labored perseveringly six months, and upwards, without a penny's return for their toil and expenses. In fact, though it should not be mentioned as an inducement to idleness, or as a principle to govern the conduct of any, it would appear that those who labored the hardest, and with the greatest perseverance, were not the most successful diamond finders. But the large ones, in many cases, were found or secured by indifferent miners, and those who were not personally engaged in searching for them, or else humbugging was carried on more extensively than I supposed.

But the great charm and attraction about the fields, and that which causes, and will continue to cause, people to go to them and try their luck, is, as some are known to be successful, the great confidence every one has in his own fortune. Each conceives, through some chance, by hook or by crook, they must obtain the gem that will give them sudden wealth. Some after a trial by weary labor for several months, the pearl of great price not appearing, as they watch for it from day to day, turn their steps homeward with sadder and, perhaps, better hearts; others, though, doubtless, few in numbers, return with wealth in their pockets and joy in their eyes.

CHAPTER IX.

THE literature of gems is already very extensive. In almost all ages of the world some author has found time and occasion for issuing a treatise, more or less extensive, upon this subject, and the writer of this little work could hardly find an excuse for attempting to force his own thoughts thereon upon the consideration of the public. Yet, believing some knowledge of precious stones in this connection would be very acceptable, I have collected together, from various sources, the matter hereinafter set forth. The following pages are not claimed to be original with the author of the foregoing narrative, either in the statement of facts, or in the theories advanced ; but unless where an opinion is given on some of the facts or theories, simply a compilation of the best writers, and the most reliable and acknowleged authority among the merchants and dealers in gems. The language of the compiler may often be used, it being unavoidable, perhaps a misfortune, when one attempts to select from other writers their various opinions and allegations. Therefore I will not charge any one with the language here employed, but the substance of what is set forth I must lay to the declarations contained in the standard works of celebrated writers on the subject. In treating of diamonds it seems difficult, if not impossible, to proceed intelligently without including in the several branches of the subject all gems recognized as precious, and for that reason all precious stones may be taken into consideration in the following chapters.

Diamonds, and other gems, were known and used in the most remote ages of antiquity of which we have any knowledge. But in the earlier periods of the world, of which there is any historical record, they appear to have been sought for and worn, more on account of some magic or talismanic properties they were supposed to possess than for the purposes of ornament.

The definition now given to the term " precious gems" is that they are minerals remarkable for hardness, lustre, beauty of color, transparency, or for the extreme rarity of their occurence in nature, and which are used in personal ornaments.

This definition excludes many gems so classed by mineralogists, but which have no commercial value.

The estimation in which these flowers of the mineral kingdom have been held in all ages of the world, alike by the most refined and the most barbarous nations, is extraordinary, so much so that gems really seem to be endowed with some occult charm which causes them to be so much coveted.

The study of the early history of precious stones, and the sources from which they were obtained, by the aid of those languages which were once spoken in the vast tracts of country situate between the Ganges and the Nile, and with the view of obtaining a knowledge of the intercourse and connection of the by-gone eastern races, must be interesting to the scholar of antiquity, and might prove useful in lifting the veil which now conceals so much of the commercial relations and communications between the extinct nations that once occupied that country and flourished in the very earliest epoch. It is not possible as yet to give a full account of the knowledge of precious stones possessed by these nations, since oriental scholars have not sufficiently occupied themselves with this subject, which might help to throw light on the state of ancient civilization, and the mechanical and artistic knowledge cultivated in those remote regions by the ancients.

In several parts of the Bible much useful information is found on this theme. According to this ancient record precious stones were not then in the possession of the majority of the opulent classes. Among the contributors of the materials towards the erection of the tabernacle, the chiefs of the twelve tribes alone are mentioned as supplying the "Shoham (onyx) stones, and the stones to be set." (Exodus xxxv., 27.) But the most important enumeration of precious stones known to the Hebrews, and mentioned in the Bible, is made in Exodus xxviii., verses 17 to 20, where Moses is commanded to "set in the breast-plate of judgment, for the high priest, settings of four rows of stones:" the first "a sardius, a topaz, and a carbuncle;" the second row "an emerald, a sapphire, and a diamond;" the third "a ligure, an agate, and an amethyst;" and the fourth "a beryl, and an onyx, and a jasper," to "be set in gold in their enclosings." And the same list is repeated in that book in the xxxix. chapter, verses 10 to 13, where it is related that the breast-plate was made as the Lord had commanded. It ought, perhaps, also to be mentioned that, with the exception of three, the gems worn by the high priest on his breast-plate were also to be found among the royal orna-ments worn by the king of Tyre (see Ezekiel xxviii., 13). In addition to the twelve stones contained in the breast-plate, the following names occur in various parts of the bible : kadkod and ekdock (Isaiah liv., 12), both of which signify the glowing of fire, and are not inappropriately translated "carbuncle." The Alexand-rian version of the Bible renders the former word 'jas-per." Ramoth, mentioned in Ezekiel xxvii., 16, and Job xxviii., 18, is of doubtful meaning, and supposed to signify coral. Gabish, or Elgabish, occurring also in the just mentioned passage of Job, means, in its primary signification, hail-stone, and hence is applied to the crystal, but according to the Chaldean paraphrase it denotes beryl. Shamir (diamond), the passage in Eze-kiel iii., 9, "as an adamant, harder than flint," etc., con-firms the supposition that shamir means diamonds. Tradition asserts that the stones which were used in the construction of the temple of So'omon were hewn by means of the shamir, as the law of Moses prohibited the use of iron implements. It must, however, be ob-served, that in this instance the word shamir has been interpreted by commentators as relating to a miraculous worm, which, being placed on the stone, performed the wonder of cleaving it in those parts which had been previously marked. We may, hereafter, have oc-casion to speak more fully of the twelve stones which were in the breast-plate of the high priest of the He-brews, but for the present we will leave the records of

7 *

the sacred volume, and see what may be gathered from later writers.

In Ancient Egypt, jewels were engraved in the form of scarabæi, and even at the present time they are disinterred from mummy pits and burial places of the ancient Egyptians.

Precious stones were no doubt brought from the East to the Egyptians and Greeks by the Phœnicians. The emerald sent from Babylon as a present to the king of Egypt, four cubits in length and three cubits in breadth, was probably green jasper; as Theophrastus, a Greek writer, mentions having seen an emerald, so-called, which was partly emerald and partly jasper. Mines of emerald, however, exist in Egypt; but they have not been worked for centuries, yet they have been visited very recently by European travellers. Gems seem to have become quite plentiful in this country in its days of greatest prosperity and advancement. Cleopatra is said to have dissolved a pearl of the value of 150,000 aureos, or golden crowns, in vinegar, in the presence of Antony, and to have drunk it off. But this must be untrue, for it would require a very much stronger acid, and a larger quantity than any one could take with impunity, to dissolve a pearl of that magnitude. Lucan mentions the meeting of Cæsar and Cleopatra in a hall of tortoise-shell, studded with emeralds and topaz. The fellow drop to the pendant destroyed by Cleopatra was sawn in two by command of the Roman Emperor, Augustus, and used to adorn the statue of Venus.

In the very earliest literature of the Greeks, we find

many notices of precious stones. Homer speaks of the ear-rings of Juno, as containing shining gems; and it is well known that the Greeks used gems for seals, rings, etc. There are still extant ancient Greek intaglei of turquoise, onyx, and also ruby ; and in a poem by Orpheus, or as some suppose, by Onomacriton, written over four hundred years before the Christian era, the supernatural power of gems, in which the Greeks had implicit belief, is mentioned.

One of their early writers ascribed to rock-crystal the power of producing the sacred fire used in the Eleusinian mysteries; the crystal was laid upon chips of wood in the rays of the sun, when first smoke and then flame was produced, and the fire thus made was believed to be the most acceptable to the gods.

A great part of the Grecian mythology was derived from the Egyptians; and as the priests were well acquainted with the use of many scientific instruments, which were carefully concealed from the vulgar, or common people, it is quite probable that this tradition arose simply from the use of glass or crystal lenses (burning glasses). Plato and Aristotle, Greek philosophers who flourished three hundred and fifty years before Christ, were both acquainted with the existence of gems; and Theophrastus, the disciple and friend of Aristotle, wrote a treatise on the subject, which is still extant.

Plato imagined the origin of precious stones to be the vivifying spirit abiding in the stars, which, longing to form new things, converts the most vile and putrid matter into the most perfect objects. He represents the diamond as being found like a kernel in the gold, and supposed it to be the purest and noblest part, which had become condensed into a transparent mass.

Theophrastus, in his theory, asserts that water is the basis of the formation of all metals, earth of all stones; that from the dissimilitude of all matter in its pristine state, and from the manner of the coalescence and concretion of different substances, the stones have taken their various qualities, such as density, transparency, smoothness, etc. This union of matter he represents being produced, in some instances, by heat, and in others by cold. The emerald, he affirms, has the property of causing water to assume its color. He speaks of a common belief, prevalent at the time of his writing, of the power of some stones to generate others, although he does not attach credence to this idea. He also describes the carbuncle found in Carthage and in Massillia as bright red, and that when held before the sun, they resembled glowing coals, which wholly corresponds with the gem now given the same name. The Greeks believed rock crystal a congelation like ice, and supposed it to be found only in the coldest regions. Theophrastus, Aristotle, and Pliny, a Roman historian who flourished in the first century of the Christian era, all concurred in this opinion.

When the Romans conquered Greece and Egypt they took home with them this taste for precious stones, and carried it to a stupendous pitch—the opulent and noble classes, and the patricians even, vieing which each other in the extravagant use of jewels. Cæsar is said to have paid a sum equal to two hundred and fifty thousand dollars for a single pearl. In later periods of

Roman history we find numberless instances of the estimation in which jewels were held. In the time of the Ptolemies they were used in profusion for ornamenting arms, drinking cups, and the altars of the gods. A poem, by Dionysius Periegetes, contains several allusions to precious stones. The asterios, whose lustre is like a star, the lychnis of the color of fire, the amethyst with a tint of purple, are all mentioned by him. Caligula is said to have adorned his horse with a collar of pearls; the shoes of Heliogabalus were studded with gems, and the statues of the gods had eyes of precious stones, a custom probably derived from the East, and which has existed there even up to the present time. One of the largest diamonds in the Russian treasury is known to have formed the eye of an idol in an eastern temple, and was stolen from it by a European who had become a priest at the shrine.

There was a belief among the Romans, that a particular stone was sacred to each month in the year, and they were called zodiac stones; they were all set together, in an ornament called an amulet, in their order, so that the one relating to each particular zodiacal sign should correspond with the proper month. The order was as follows:

January.........Aquarius..Jacinth or Garnet.
February.........Pisces.........Amethyst.
March..........Aries.........Bloodstone.
April...........Taurus........Sapphire.
May............Gemini........Agate.
June............Cancer........Emerald.
July............Leo..........Onyx.

August..........Virgo.........Cornelian.
September........Libra.........Chrysalite.
October..........Scorpio........Aquamarine.
November........Sagittarius.....Topaz.
December.........Capricorn......Ruby.

The superstition of the Romans may be connected
with the twelve stones in the breast-plate of the High
Priest of the Hebrews. However, it still exists. There
was a tradition among the Jews, that on the day of
atonement, when the High-Priest asked the Almighty
forgiveness for the sins of the whole nation, if God
was inclined to grant the request, the stones in the
Urim and Thummim shone mostly brightly ; if, on the
contrary, they were not forgiven, the stones became
black.

In the Hindoo mythology, gems are spoken of in a
manner which shows that they were held in general estimation among that people. In their songs and bal-·
lads precious stones are frequently mentioned, and
Pliny records that the garments and utensils of the Indian
nations were ornamented with jewels, which practice, no
doubt, was of the greatest antiquity. With what stones
these eastern people were acquainted is not known,as the
names given them, both in the Scriptures and in other
early accounts, differ from those used at the present
time ; and in fact the only stone of whose identity with
one mentioned in the holy-writ there is any certainty, is
the sapphire, as it bears the same name in Hebrew
(ספיר), and is described as a transparent blue stone,
"like unto the vault of heaven." But this even could
not have been the sapphire of the Greeks and Romans,

which they represent as intermixed with gold. Tavernier gives the first authentic account of the jewels existing in India. He relates what he saw in his journeys to that country. But in speaking of what was told him, he falls into many exaggerations.

In the buried cities of Pompeii and Herculaneum there have been found rings engraved with devices on green jasper and chalcedony.

Juba, king of Mauritania, is said to have had a statue, four cubits long, made of one single piece of chrysalite, which he presented to Arsinoë, the wife of Ptolemy. Coming down to still later periods, the conquerors of Mexico and Peru found the Montezumas and the Incas in possession of gems, engraved and cut into the forms of animals and other objects to which their traditions gave a remote antiquity. Of the countries in which jewels are worn and used at the present time, it is unnecessary to speak, for it would include every inhabited part of the globe, the civilized and enlightened as well as the uncivilized. Barbarous and savage nations all have a great love for these ornaments, and the preceding account is considerable proof that they have been known and prized in all ages and by nearly every race of men. Consequently their first discovery and existence is lost far back in the unrecorded events, or mythological superstition of the first generations of the human family.

. The superstitious belief of the ancients, that their gems possessed certain talismanic properties, is quite clearly shown in the writings already referred to. This belief is shared more or less by almost every nation,

and at the present time it is not extinct, even in the
most enlightened nations, and many persons now wear
a turquoise with the supposition that it saves them from
contagion.   Gems were likewise believed to indicate
the state of the health of the donor or possessor.   If
they became dull, he was conjectured to be unwell or in
danger ; and their becoming opaque or colorless, would
give rise to the most dismal forebodings.

The turquoise, among the ancients, was conceived to
have an affinity with its possessor, or master, and to
change its color as his state of health varied.   This notion
may be accounted for, from the fact that some turquoises
do change their color ; the real cause of their varying hue
seems to arise from the difference of temperature, and
from the state of the weather.

The knowledge of the properties of gems common to
the writers of the middle ages differs but little from that
declared by Pliny and Aristotle.   Marbodus, Boetius,
Cardanus, and Rhave adopted the statements of
Pliny in many instances; and Thomas Nicolls, in a
book written by him, published at Cambridge, England,
in the year 1652 A.D., quotes the affirmations of Pliny,
and Theophrastus, about the diamond, as being perfectly true.

Albertus Magnus, Longius, Cardanus, Boetius, and
others, have written at length on this subject, and their
speculations as to the origin of gems, and their supernatural effects, are very amusing.   Scrapius ascribes to
the diamond the power of driving away lemures, incu-
bes, and succubes, and of making men courageous and
magnanimous, and asserts that loadstone placed with

the gem nullifies its power. Boetius in his work "De Natura Gemmarum," declares the ruby to be a sovereign remedy against the plague and poison; it also, according to this writer, drives away evil spirits and bad dreams, The jacinth, worn on the finger, procures sleep, and brings riches, honor, and wisdom. The amethyst dispels drunkenness, and sharpens the wit. He says of the balas-ruby, that it restrains passion, and fiery wrath, and is a preservative from lightning; of the emerald, that it discovered false witnesses by suffering changes when it met with such persons; the sapphire procured favor with princes, and delivered from enchantments; the chrysolite was said to cool boiling water, and assuage wrath, and if placed in contact with poison to lose its brilliancy until removed. He supposed gems to be generated by the powerful working of lapidific spirits, and enlarged by the acquisition of new matter; and that the pearl was formed by the morning dew, drank in by shell-fish. The twelve apostles were symbolized by certain stones: Peter is represented by the jasper; Andrew, by sapphire; James, chalcedony; John, emerald; Philip, sardonyx; Bartholomew, cornelian; Matthew, chrysolite; Thomas, beryl; Thaddeus, chrysoprase; James the Lesser, topaz; Simeon, jacinth; and Matthias by the amethyst.

Some gems powdered were also used in ancient times for medical purposes, and considered almost infallible in their effects. And even at the present time large quantities of seed pearl are used in China and the east for various medicinal remedies.

In a curious medical treatise, written by Antonius

Musa Brassarobus, lapis lazuli is prescribed as a laxative. Camillus Leonardus, of Pisa, recommends coral in powder for newly-born children. The natives of India imagine that diamond dust taken into the mouth causes the teeth to drop out, and also that it is a preservative against lightning, and they believe some stones give light in the dark. The Vedas of the Brahmins speak of a place "illuminated by rubies and diamonds" which emit light like that of the planets.

If such superstitious theories were taught, as appears by the writings of the most learned men of their times, among nearly every people, it cannot be considered strange that the most extravagant and absurd notions should have prevailed among the ignorant. Indeed, at first thought, it would seem that these scholars must have known better, and that they disseminated such opinions and doctrines for the purpose of working upon the ignorance and superstition of their fellow creatures to their own advantage; but when we consider, comparatively, the little advancement that had then been made in the sciences, and the darkness that, at best, surrounded the pathway, even of the greatest philosophers and most learned scholars, and think of the rapid strides in knowledge made in the last centuries, while even yet some people are ever ready to grasp at the marvellous, and to believe it miraculous or supernatural, it is not difficult to conclude that these writers transcribed their true belief, and advanced theories, which, from their honest convictions, were correct. When chemistry, however, began to be understood, the ideas which had been handed down by tradition and by the works of ancient authors, were proved erroneous, and the clouds which hung over the subject were dispelled by the analysis and classification of gems, according to their composition, hardness, lustre, etc., the old system of classing all stones of similar color together was abandoned. Therefore, in modern times, great light has been thrown on the subject of the formation of precious stones by the researches of learned chemists and mineralogists. Yet, although there has been great advancement in the sciences, and our means of obtaining knowledge are far more extended and voluminous than that of our ancestors, still there is much to be learned in the wide field of geology, and possibly we may find that future inquiry will reveal to the world that the opinions and theories of the present age are as unsound and erroneous as those entertained in more primitive periods.

CHAPTER X.

PRECIOUS stones are disseminated about the globe in considerable profusion. They occur alike in the torrid deserts of Africa, and the icy steppes of Siberia; under the burning sun of India and Ceylon, and amidst the glaciers of Switzerland; in the beds of the mighty rivers of South America, and sometimes on the very summits of lofty mountains—in Germany, Spain, England, and America, generally surrounded by some substance or deposits differing entirely from them. They are found in the greatest abundance, however, in the tropical countries. It would seem as if those parts of the earth on which the sun shines with the greatest splendor produce these beautiful creations of nature in the largest quantities; perhaps the volcanic changes to which these lands are subject may have something to do with their creation or exposure. They likewise appear to exist most frequently in the older formations, such as granite, gneiss, etc., as though only the operations of eternal ages could bring them forth. In the beds of rivers they are generally accompanied by the precious metals, and various kinds of gems are often found together. But when all the circumstances and wonderful combinations, which are required to form these beautiful crystals, to give them their transparency, brilliancy, and lustre, freedom from defects, and the coloring matter to produce the desired tint, are considered, it is no occasion for wonder that they occur so seldom. Although the minerals, which are the component parts of this aristocratic family are plentiful throughout the earth, magnesia, glucina, alumina, metallic oxides, etc., can be obtained in abundance, and carbon, the material of the diamond, is found almost everywhere—in the bread we eat and the coals we burn—and although the gems themselves can be separated into their various parts. yet no one has yet succeeded in wresting from nature the secret of combining these materials so as to form the beautiful stones; and none of any size or value have ever been produced by artificial means.

The diamond, the first in rank above all others, the gem of gems, is found in Hindostan, Brazil, Sumatra, Borneo, the Ural Mountains, occasionally in North America, in some instances in Australia and in Africa. Ordinarily it occurs in strata of plutonic origin in octahedral crystals, in quartz containing oxides of iron ; also in alluvium in loose and imbedded crystals, but almost always of a smaller size, and very frequently in company with grains of gold and platinum.

In India, the localities where this stone is obtained were in the Deccan, the river Pennair in the lower Kistna, and Ellore, and Pannah, and the river Sonar, and some were found in the Bundlecund, at Sumbhulpore on the Mahanuddy; also Malacca, Celebes and Java have yielded up their wealth in this jewel. But India, which used to be the great source of diamonds, seems to have become gradually exhausted ; and many places where they were formerly found became so unproductive that not only the localities themselves, but their very names, are unknown to the present inhabitants of that country. According to Tavernier, a French jeweler, and trustworthy authority, who travelled in the East and through Hindostan in the seventeenth century, the mines of Golconda then employed 60,000 persons, and were once so productive that, as is recorded by the historian Ferichta, the Sultan Mahmoud (A.D. 1177-1206) left in his treasures, after a reign of thirty-two years, more than four hundred pounds' weight of this precious gem.

In Sumbhulpore the diamond-washing trade is hereditary in two tribes, whose origin is unknown, but who appear, from the traces of negro blood, to be descendants of slaves imported by one of the conquerors of India for that labor. They are called respectively Thara and Tora, and possess sixteen villages in free Jhager or freehold. They number 400 or 500 persons, working in the dry season in the bed of the Mahanuddy, from Kunderpore to Sinepore. The largest diamond found there since the transfer of the country from the Maharatta to British rule was one of eighty-four grains. The Indians call the diamond "pakha," or ripe, and rock crystal "Kacha," or unripe.

Brazil, at the present time, far surpasses India in the production of this jewel. In Brazil they are found chiefly in alluvial soil in the districts of San Paulo, Cerro di Fria, and Minas Geraes; in the beds of the rivers Matto Grasso, Jequitinhonha, in Diamantina, Rio des Areios, Santa Anna, Paulo Vehas, San Francisco, Rio Sumedouro, Bahia, San Francisco di Xavier, and other places. Diamonds were discovered in Brazil when searching for gold, but for some time their true nature was not known by the inhabitants, and they were thrown away as worthless, or used only as counters for card-players, and for dice. Bernardo Fonseca Labo, an inhabitant of the Minas Geraes, who had seen rough diamonds in a previous visit to the East Indies, first disclosed their true nature and value. A large quantity of them was gathered up and taken to Lisbon, and their identity fully established.

European traders, fearing their stock in this gem would be depreciated, and, perhaps, become nearly valueless, if a large number was brought into market by this discovery of new mines, circulated a report that the so-called Brazilian diamonds were only the refuse of the East India mines, which had been exported from Goa to Brazil and then sent to Europe. David Jeffries, who was the great authority in Europe on the subject of diamonds and pearls, published a book about this time (A.D. 1750), in which he endorses the report, and even tries to prove its truth by argument; every means was devised to prevent their sale, and at first with considerable success. The Portuguese merchants, however, under the maxim of "diamond cut diamond," exported their jewels from Brazil to Goa, and then offering them for sale as Indian gems turned the tables on the European traders.

The miners in Brazil distinguish the different diamond-producing soils by the following names: Grupiara, Burgalhao, Takoa Carza, and Cascalho.

Grupiara is an alluvial deposit, and is probably the
unused bed of a stream or river.

Cascalho consists of fragments of rock mixed with
sand and clay, and forming the bed of a river; Cascalho
is also a generic name applied to all the soils.

Burgalhao are small angular fragments of rock which
bestrew the surface of the ground, and

Takoa Carza are all the foregoing substances cement-
ed together in one mass.

In the Itambe mountain, the highest in the district,
and in which the rivers Copay and Jequitinhonha rise,
diamonds are sometimes found even on its very peaks,
5,598 feet above the level of the sea. The wealth of
the Brazilian mines is incalculable; it is said the gold
is abandoned to the slaves as unworthy the attention of
their owners; and children, after the rains, collect the
grains of gold which have become exposed to view.
The crops of all fowls killed are carefully examined, and
frequently found to contain diamonds; and it is recorded
that a negro once found a stone of five carats adhering
to the roots of a cabbage he had plucked for his dinner.
A slave, who had been working at the mines in Minas
Geraes, and in 1754 transferred to the district of
Bahia, believing from the similarity of the soil with that
of the place he had left that it contained diamonds,
searched and found a considerable quantity. This news
becoming public, that province was inundated with
emigrants seeking to make rapid fortunes, in the same
manner as the tide of population flowed to California or
Australia when the gold discoveries in those countries

were made known. The production of the Brazils in these gems has been very great. It is estimated that the astonishing amount of sixty million dollars in value was exported the first fifty years after their discovery. The yield of the Bahia mines was at first so considerable as to reduce the value of the diamond one-half; but the supply is said to have gradually decreased, and is growing less every year. The total produce does not now exceed 240,000 carats yearly. The richest mines at the present time are in the province of Matto-Grosso, near the town of Diamantina.

The discovery of diamonds in Brazil seemed at first to act as a curse on the inhabitants of the districts where they were found. As soon as the government learned the wealth of the treasures within its grasp, it took possession of the land, expelled the inhabitants, declared the trade a monopoly, and it the exclusive proprietors. Nature even seemed to have a spite against the expatriated exiles. The first year the whole district was subjected to a dreadful drought, and, to add to the distress of the unfortunate people, a fearful earthquake took place, by which numbers of them perished. It appeared as though the genii, guardians of the treasures, were indignant at the presumption of man, and tried by every means to prevent the dispersion of their buried treasures, or to wreak vengeance on the disturbers of their most inviolable dominions. But in May, 1803, the sad remnant of the original inhabitants were reinstated in their rightful property.

The mode of washing for diamonds here is somewhat different from the description heretofore given of that in

8

Southern Africa. When the rivers are the lowest in the dry season, which lasts from April to the middle of October, their waters are diverted from the natural channels into canals dug for the purpose, leaving the bed of the stream dry. The soil is then taken out, to the depth of ten or twelve feet, and placed near the washing-huts. This labor is continued during the whole of the dry season, after which, when the rains have so swollen the rivers as to prevent the diversion of the water, the washing of the cascalho commences. The huts are furnished with long troughs or canoes. and elevated seats for the overseers. The laborers, who are negroes, fill the trough with the soil, when a stream of water is allowed to run in and off while they continue to stir the mass until the water runs clear, and all the earthy particles are washed away. They then examine the pebbles, one by one, and if a diamond is found, give the signal by clapping their hands, when the overseer takes it and places it in a vessel filled with water, one of which hangs suspended in the centre of each hut. At the conclusion of the day's labor the weight produced is entered in a book. It is said the cascalho contains diamonds in so regular proportions that the miners are able to tell, with considerable certainty, what any given quantity will produce. Large diamonds are very rare ; on an average, a gem of eighteen carats is not found in these mines in every 10,000. When a slave finds one of eighteen carats' weight, or upwards, he is led, crowned with flowers, in a kind of triumphal procession, to the proprietor, who grants him his freedom, and usually gives him a present, and allows him thereafter to work on his own account. For smaller stones less rewards are given. The largest gem ever found in Brazil is the "Star of the South," which weighed 254 carats, and is hereafter more particularly mentioned under the head of Large Diamonds.

Notwithstanding the many precautions that are taken, thefts are sometimes committed by the slaves, even under the very eye of the overseer. The laborer will conceal a stone in his hair, mouth, or ear, or between his fingers or toes, and they have been known to throw them away in the hope of finding them again after nightfall. When the labor and pains bestowed in this search for diamonds is remembered, the result appears scarcely commensurate with the toil. The product of the work of 500 men for a year can be readily carried in the hand. The miner having secured a sufficient quantity, he sends them to Rio Janeiro; this takes a considerable time, as the distance is great, and the roads lie through endless primeval forests. In Rio they are sold to the merchant, who ships them to Europe, or holds them, as the price and demand may induce him to act.

In Borneo diamonds are found in the chain of mountains which borders the great river Banger, principally in the district of Jannah-Laut; here, too, they are accompanied by grains of gold. The mines in this island employ about 400 persons, and the search is in much the same manner as in other places. These gems are likewise found in the island of Sumatra, in Java, and in the Ural mountains in the Russian Empire. Crystals of diamonds have been obtained in Australia, but of too

isolated occurrence to warrant its being classed as a diamond-producing country.   Of the mines of South Africa
it is unnecessary further to speak.

The ruby, sapphire, oriental topaz, etc., all properly
corundums, being identical in every particular but that
of color, which difference may be said to be the only
cause for giving each a name.   The red sapphire is a
ruby, the blue ruby a sapphire, the yellow a topaz, etc.
The word corundum, however, is of Indian origin, derived from the sanskrit "Korund," and is only applied
to the opaque varieties, which present the characteristic
hexagonal crystals, but of a dull color.   Rubies are
found associated with sapphires, magnetic iron, zircons,
oxides of tin, spinels, rutile, topaz, etc., usually in hexagonal, rounded prisms, in layers in the earth, and beds
of rivers, in various parts of the globe, almost always
accompanied with gold.

The finest rubies are obtained in the kingdom of Ava,
in Siam, in the Capelan mountains, ten days' journey
from Syrian, a city in Pegu.   They are also found in
Ceylon, at Hohenstein on the Elbe, in Hindostan, in the
Rhine and Danube rivers, in Brazil, Borneo, Sumatra,
Australia, in France, in the rivers Espailly, Auvergne,
and Iser, in Bohen ia, etc., etc.   The ruby mines of
Burmah have long been known, and the king of the
country is said to possess the rarest and most wonderful specimens.   These mines are scrupulously guarded,
and a foreigner is not allowed to approach them on any
pretense.   They are a royal monopoly, and the order is
to retain all for the king's treasury.   When a large,
fine stone is found, it is customary to send out a proces-

sion of grandees, with soldiers and elephants, to meet it, and escort it to the royal presence with great ceremony. One of the titles of the king is "Lord of the Rubies." These mines are worked by sinking shafts until the ruby-producing soil is met with, which in some places is two, and in others thirty feet or upwards below the surface. When the proper stratum is found it is followed and worked until it becomes necessary to sink another shaft, or until it is exhausted. The gems are most always small, and seldom free from defects. Rhombohedral crystals are rarely perfect, and usually worn into rounded surfaces. Rubies are also found in Ceylon, in the beds of rivers, and occasionally some fine stones are sent from that island; but the blue variety, the sapphire, is more frequently met with there, and the crystals are of a much larger size than those in Burmah. Specimens have likewise been obtained in Australia, but of poor quality.

The sapphire, which is like the ruby, except in color, as before remarked, is found chiefly in Ceylon, where the red stone is seldom obtained. It generally occurs in crystals of larger size than the ruby, and is very rarely to be met with in minute crystals.

The chrysoberyl, also called oriental chrysolite, a very brilliant gem, of a yellow, perhaps inclining to green, brown or red color, and occasionally white, is obtained in rounded pebbles in the alluvial deposits of rivers in Ceylon, near Saffragang in Moravia, in the Rio Americanus, and Rio Piantie of Brazil, in the Tajowaja of the Ural Mountains. It has also been found at Haddam, Connecticut; at Greenfield, near Saratoga, New

York; and in the granite of Orange Summit, Vermont.

Balas ruby, and spinel, which terms include spinel ruby, rubicelle, almandine ruby, also an opaque variety called ceylonite or pleonast, the chloro (green) spinel, the sapphirine (blue), the dyshnite, the hercenite, etc., are procured from granular limestones, and with calcareous spar in Ava, Mysore, Beloochistan, Ceylon, and other Eastern countries, in alluvial deposits and beds of rivers. In the countries named, the finest specimens are obtained which are used for jewelry.

Pale blue spinel (sapphirine) is found at Aher in Sweden, in Farland and Straskau, Moravia. Black crystals of considerable lustre are found with mica and garnet in old lava on Mount Somma, the chloro (green) spinel in slate at Slatonht, Ural mountains, its green color being, doubtless, chargeable to the presence of peroxide of iron. The black pleonast or ceylonite is procured in Bohemia, Ceylon, in the river Iser, in the Tyrol, at Andernach on the Rhine, and in many places in the United States where brown spinels are plentiful. Sweden furnishes automalite or zinc spinel. A white kind occurs at La Riccia, near Rome, in Italy. Marco Polo, in his Travels, speaks of the "*rubis-balais*" (balas ruby) as being chiefly found in the mountains called Shek·nim. The Persians, even up to the present time, have preserved a tradition that these gems were not discovered until after an earthquake which rent the mountain in twain; and that they were at first mistaken for true rubies, but their inferior hardness made known the error. Balas ruby is the ancient name of Beloochistan, Balaschan, or Badakschan; the Persian name is Badakschiani. Sebaldus Ravius, an ancient author, observes : "Nomen ejus balachsch diciturque a Teifaschio adduci ex Balachschano, quam regionem barbari Badackschan vocant, estque secundum eum pars terrae Turcarum, quae ad Tartarium vergit." The Greeks thought the name derived from Balassus, or Palassus, supposed to be the place in which the true ruby dwelt.

Topaz is found in almost every part of the world in granite and gneiss rocks which contain fluor spar, but varying in color and aspect in almost every different location. In Villa Rica, Brazil, this stone has a brownish-yellow hue, and is obtained from a loose sandy soil, which renders the search a very easy task. It also comes from the Minas Geraes, pure and colorless, bearing a high degree of polish ; and similar specimens are found in Tasmania, with blue and green. Those of a fine pale blue are brought from Siberia, Alabascka, Murinsk, Odentochelong and Miask ; of a pure yellow from Altenburg in Saxony ; also Ceylon, Peru, Asia Minor, Connecticut in the United States, Ireland, Scotland, England, and the Hebrides produce the topaz.

The emerald, a stone unsurpassed by any other gem for its beautiful green color, crystallized in regular hexagonal prisms, to which system it belongs, is unearthed at Muzo, in New Grenada, near Santa Fé de Bogota, from a limestone rock. These mines are let by the government for a term of years by public tender ; they formerly produced an annual revenue of a sum equal to $40,000, but at the expiration of the term of rental the lessees declined to continue the contract at

the same price. Parisite, a rare mineral of a brown hexagonal crystal, opaque, is also found at this place. The
emerald is likewise met with at Henbachthal, in Salz-
burg, imbedded in mica slate, on a steep precipice 8,700
feet above the level of the sea, and only accessible by
means of ropes. It is also found at Odentochelong, in
Siberia, in the Burman Empire near Ava. And an
ancient emerald mine, with large galleries, bearing the
marks of the miners' tools and their ancient appliances.
such as levers, etc., was discovered by Monsieur Cail-
land, a French traveller, in the mountains of Zabareh.
when he was on a scientific excursion for the Pasha of
Egypt.

The beryl, or aquamarine, is more generally obtained
than the emerald. Splendid specimens are procured in
Siberia. It is also found at Invercauld and Kinloch
Rannoch, Scotland; and in the Mourne mountains,
county of Down, in Glen Macnah, county of Wicklow,
at Dalkey and Three Rock Mountains, county of
Dublin, Ireland; at Limoges, France; at Bodenmais
and Rabenstein, Bavaria; at Fimbo and Brodbo, in
Sweden; in Saxony; Bohemia; the Isle of Elba; in
Norway; Finland; the Rio San Matheo, Brazil; in
Hindostan, and in some parts of the United States.

An enormous beryl is said to have been discovered
in Massachusetts, weighing five tons, but has never
been removed from its location.

Zircon, hyacinth, or jacinth, is found in imbedded
and attached crystals, in granite, syenite, and gneiss, in
beds of rivers, often with garnets ; in the East Indies,
Ceylon, New Granada, France, Bohemia, and in North

America. Specimens have also been found in the lava of Vesuvius.

Garnets are obtained in India, Pegu, Ceylon, Brazil, in the Tyrol, in Sweden, Arendal, Norway, Bohemia, Saxony, Siberia, and other countries. It is a gem distributed very generally in almost every part of the world. It is found imbedded in mica, slate, granite, gneiss, limestone, chlorite, serpentine, lava, etc.

Tourmaline, but little used for jewelry, can be procured in Ceylon, Ava, Siberia, Brazil, Bavaria, the United States, Greenland, England, and in the island of Elba.

Quartz, which includes amethyst, cairngorm, cat's-eye, onyx, cornelian, chrysoprase, sardonyx, chalcedony, agate, jasper, mocha-stone, blood-stone, aventurine, rock crystal, etc., are obtained in various localities—some in almost every country, while others are less generally disseminated. It is thought hardly neccessary to name every place in which each may be met with, and hereafter some mention may be made of their several localities.

The turquoise of commerce comes from Nichabour, in Khorasan, in Persia. An inferior quality is found in Thibet, China, Siberia, and at Oelnitz in Saxony, and not long since there has been discovered a new variety in Arabia Petræa, near Mount Sinai in a strata of red sandstone.

Opal, which really belongs to the family of quartz, yet being a splendid gem, is procured in claystone porphyry at Czernowitza, between Kaschanc and Eperies, in Hungary; in the province of Gracias, Honduras, South America; and sometimes near Frankfort. Fire opal is

8 *

obtained at Zimopan, and San Nicholas, Mexico, in the Faroe Islands, and other places. The common opal is found in Hungary, Faroe Islands, in Cornwall, England, and near Smyrna.

Pearl, a beautiful gem formed by nature in the shells of oysters and mussels, is obtained in the beds of rivers and in the sea, in numerous places, in and near Europe, Asia, and America. The principal pearl fisheries are in the east, on the west coast of Ceylon, in the Bay of Manaar, in the Persian Gulf, and near the Sooloo Islands.

Pearl fishing is also carried on in the Aroo Islands, near the Island of Papua or New Guinea, in the Red Sea, in America, on both the Atlantic and Pacific coasts.

In Ceylon, the pearl fishery is owned and carried on by the government. When the period to work at the oyster beds arrives, and after the natives who are employed in this business have performed their numerous ceremonies on the shore, they set out with a fleet of boats, perhaps over a hundred, under the command of an adanapar, or chief pilot. Each boat is manned with twenty men, besides a steersman, and a pillal karras (shark charmer), ten rowers, and ten divers. The pillal karras are regularly employed by the government, and sent out with each boat, as the divers would not descend into the sea without their presence. There are other conjurers also who mutter incantations on the shore till the boats return. On the side of each boat a stage is constructed, from which the divers drop into the water.

When they have arrived at the fisheries, the divers go
down into the sea, five at a time from each crew ; after
the first five come up, the others descend, while the first
are preparing for another plunge, and so on, each set
continuing to dive alternately as the other rises till the
day's work is done.   In order to quicken their descent,
a large stone weighing about twenty-five pounds is used.
It is commonly of a reddish granite, of a pyramidal form,
rounded at the top and bottom, and has a hole in the
small end by which to attach a rope.   Some divers use
a stone of a half-moon shape fastened round the waist.
When all else is prepared the diver seizes the rope, to
which one of the stones is fastened, with the toes of his
right foot, and with those of his left a bag of net work.
From custom and the power of habit they use their toes
in holding and working almost as well as their fingers,
and can pick up the smallest thing with them as nimbly
as possible.   Taking another rope in his right hand,
and holding his nostrils with his left, he plunges into the
sea.   The weight of the stone speedily brings him to
the bottom; with great dexterity and all possible dispatch
he collects as many oysters as he can during the time
he is able to remain under water, which is usually about
two minutes; he then resumes his former position, gives
the signal to those above in the boat by pulling the rope
in his right hand, and is at once drawn up.   Although
from one to two minutes is the time generally passed
under water, yet sometimes they stay four or five, and
even six minutes below the surface.   The serious effects of this continual submersion are shown in the dis-
charge of water, and occasionally blood, from the diver's

mouth, ears and nose. But it does not hinder the men from going down again in their turn, and each will make from forty to fifty descents in a day, and bring up about one hundred oysters each time. Some of the divers bathe their bodies in oil, and fill the ears and nostrils with cotton, to keep the water out, while others use no protection.

The natives stand in great fear of the ground shark, a common inhabitant of the seas in the latitude of Ceylon. If an alarm be given by one, none of the others will descend again the same day. During the time of fishing, conjurors are on the shore mumbling prayers, twisting their bodies into strange attitudes, and performing heathenish ceremonies, but sometimes regaling themselves with strong drink until no longer able to perform their devotions.

But now diving bells are beginning to be used in these fisheries, and will soon, doubtless, with similar inventions, come into general use for the purposes of descent into the water. When the day's work is done and the boats return to the shore, the oysters are taken out and placed in pits or closed vessels to putrify, after which the pearls are washed from the decayed matter in a trough or tub. Sometimes the shells are opened immediately, and the pearls extracted. Generally the oysters are sold unopened, and their contents being unknown either to seller or buyer, the transaction takes much the form of a lottery, and, in fact, the trade has in it a good deal of the spirit of gambling. Many oysters contain no pearl, whilst others may produce a gem worth $1,000 or $2,000.

The government derives quite a large revenue from this fishery, and protects it by strict regulations. The beds are carefully examined from time to time by experienced divers, and their localities buoyed out before the boats leave the land. Some time since, the supply was diminishing at the place under consideration so rapidly that it was deemed expedient to discontinue the fishery for a number of years, to prevent the beds from becoming entirely exhausted.

In the Persian Gulf the process is carried on in exactly the same manner as at Ceylon. Here, however, besides the shark, the diver has to contend with the sword-fish, which are fully as dangerous. In ancient times these fisheries were known to the Macedonians, and Seleucus, king of Syria, gave the revenues derived from them to one of his satraps. A number of years ago the Portuguese government had possession of the Persian Gulf fisheries, but I believe they are now owned by native rulers, and as many as 30,000 persons are employed in them; the gems are said to be inferior, however, to those found at Ceylon. The pearls obtained on the coast of the Zulu Islands are principally sold in China.

The Red Sea fisheries, which were immensely productive in the time of the Ptolemies, are now nearly exhausted, and yield very few pearls. Large quantities of pearls are now obtained from Panama and California. The fisheries on the coasts of these countries were doubtless known to the ancient Mexicans, for the old Spanish histories inform us that the Aztec kings had immense numbers of fine pearls in their possession, and were well acquainted with the sources whence they came. The palace of Montezuma is said to have been studded with emeralds and pearls, and the Spaniards, by their conquests of Mexico and Peru, came into possession of large quantities of this gem. Pearls are also found in the mussel-shells in rivers in Scotland, Germany, Russia, Sweden, and France, but usually of a dull leaden hue, with no lustre, and are termed Scotch pearls.

There are many other substances used in jewelry not properly precious stones, such as moon-stone, malachite, lapis-lazuli, jet, jade or nephite, labradorite or Labrador felspar, amber, coral, etc.

Moon-stone is obtained in Siberia and Ceylon.

Lapis-lazuli in Persia, Beloochistan, China, Bucharia, Siberia and Chili.

Malachite in Siberia, Burra-Bura, Australia, Africa, Cornwall, Hungary, and the Tyrol.

Labradorite in Labrador, Canada, Norway, Sweden, and some in the lava of Ætna and Vesuvius.

Jet, in clay on the coast of Yorkshire, England, on the Baltic coast, in the forest of Ardennes, and in the Pyrenees.

Jade, or nephite, in Egypt, Corsica, New Zealand, North America and China.

Amber in abundance on the Prussian coast of the Baltic, from Dantzig to Memel; on the coast of Denmark, in Sweden, Norway, Moravia, Poland, Switzerland, France, England, Asia and the United States.

Coral, the production of gelatinous mollusks of the family "polypi," forms submarine forests of leafless

branches in many parts of the globe. In the southern
hemispheres they increase so rapidly and to such an
extent, as occasionally to form islands and obstruct nav-
igation. Coral was formerly believed to be of vegetable origin on account of its growth and form; but
naturalists have identified the form of the minute insects which produce this natural phenomonon. These
polypi are shaped as an eight-pointed star, notched on
each point, with the mouth in the centre, and seem to
have an organization of sensitiveness common to all on
the same branch of coral; if one be disturbed, the
others are equally affected, so that the separate mollusks on the same branch appear to form one body. In
some respects these insects vary in different localities.
Coral islands and reefs are now known to be the work
of these little animals.

Although this substance is found in the seas of many
parts of the world, yet that which is adopted for purposes of ornament is found almost entirely in the Med-
iterranean, principally on the African coast, at a considerable depth in the sea, sometimes seven hundred or
eight hundred feet beneath the surface, which makes
the operation of fishing for it very difficult and slow.
The industry is of French origin. In 1450, a French
establishment at Calle carried on the business, bound
by the condition of employing only provincial sailors.
In 1791, the trade was thrown open to all. In 1794,
however, a duty was laid on all ships foreign to France.
At the present time the business is carried on mostly by
Italians and Maltese. Upwards of one hundred and
fifty barques are engaged every season in these fisheries.

Large quantities of coral are yearly exported to China, India and Persia, in which countries it is ranked as one of the most precious productions of nature. For further information in reference to these substances, the reader is referred to the chapter devoted to the discussion of the properties and characteristics of precious stones.

CHAPTER XI.

In order that the properties of precious stones here-inafter given may be better understood, it may be necessary, in the first instance, to define and explain some of the terms applied to them, such as hardness, lustre, specific gravity, transparency, etc.

By hardness is meant, not difficulty of breakage, but the resistance one body offers to the mechanical pressure of another, or its liability or non-liability to scratch. Moh, a German author, has furnished a mineralogical scale of hardness to be applied to precious stones. By him ten different substances are taken as standards of so many distinct degrees of hardness, and classed in numbers from one to ten: ten being the diamond the hardest known body.

On the other hand, as glass and quartz, or rock-crystals are easily obtained, and most gems are of equal or superior hardness; they are described as scratching or being scratched by them. But in trying stones, after they are cut by scratching, it must be remembered that from some extraneous cause, such as flaws or imperfect crystallization, one part may be softer than the other. In direct proportion to the hardness of a crystalized mineral is its susceptibility of receiving and retaining a good polish; and that is the chief cause of the superior brilliancy and beauty of jewels over all

other natural ornaments worn as decorations.   It is this
quality also that preserves them from the effects of
time, so visible on all the other works of nature or art.
Where the original beauty of ancient architectural remains has long since faded away, jewels of the same
date have remained untarnished by the hand of time,
and in their beauty and splendor handed down from
generation to generation, forming links in the chain of
history which, but for them, might have been lost for
ever.   The gems found in the buried cities of Pompeii
and Herculaneum, and in the catacombs of Egypt
have not been without their uses to the student
of history.

The term lustre is applied to the peculiar brilliancy
of gems, and its different kinds are called by names
corresponding to the appearances presented.   Mineralogists class the various kinds of lustre as follows :

Adamantine : possessing the brilliancy of the diamond.

Vitreous : resembling the surface of glass.

Resinous : shining as if rubbed with an oily substance.

Pearly : exhibiting the peculiar lustre of the pearl.

Silky : having a fibrous reflection similar to silk.

There is another lustre called metallic, but it is not
possessed by any precious stones.   In speaking of the
lustre of gems, the name applied must be taken as
general, and as describing as nearly as possible the appearance of each kind.

Color is a characteristic by which gems cannot be clas-
sified or identified with any degree of certainty.   They

may have the same color, yet differ in hardness, specific
gravity, etc., qualities more distinguishing in their na
ture. The ruby, spinelle, and garnet are often of exactly
similar tints; yet on this qualification, as much as on any
other, depends the commercial value of precious stones,
and their form, brilliancy, or purity is of little avail if
the color be not of the required hue.   The coloring
matter in gems chiefly arises from the presence of metallic oxides, without which they would be clear like
rock-crystal.   Sometimes the color which tinges the
whole stone is found to consist of a small speck of matter which is only visible when it is held before the
light in a particular way.   The lapidary, in such cases,
will diffuse the hue throughout the gem by means of repeated internal reflection.   The colors of precious
stones are the most brilliant in nature with which we
are acquainted, and appear more like those exhibited
by the solar spectrum than that of any other known
bodies   Color frequently changes the commercial
name of gems.   Red sapphire is a ruby; yellow, a topaz; white emerald is a beryl; green chrysolite is
called a peridot; and quartz changes its name and value
as the colors which tint it differ.   There are also gra-
dations of, and sometimes two or three different colors
in, the same specimen.   Oriental sapphires are found
with a shade of red, blue, and yellow in the same crystal; tourmalines likewise parti-colored in the most
eccentric manner.   Some gems exhibit a different color
by transmitted light from that of reflected light ; that
is, when looked through, and looked at.   The opal and
tourmaline are obtained possessing this peculiarity.

The specific gravity of a stone is the proportion its weight bears to that of an equal volume of water, and is ascertained by first weighing it in the air and then in water, subtracting the weight in water from the weight in the air, and dividing the weight in the air by the difference. For the purposes of accuracy, the substance of which the specific gravity is required must be clean, free from dust or grease, or any foreign substance, and rubbed in the water before being weighed in it to remove all the adherent air; and, if porous, must be allowed to absorb as much water as possible before being weighed in it. To know the specific gravity of a gem is of great importance; it often affords a test of the greatest value, and prevents the possibility of one gem being substituted for another when their specific gravity differs; as, for instance, a jargoon or white sapphire for diamond, which has been done by error or fraud.

There is a number of valuable instruments, such as the hydrometer, used for determining the specific gravity in scientific experiments where great accuracy is required. This test was well known by the ancients, and was practiced in India many centuries ago.

Precious stones also possess optical properties; the most important, and those which in many cases serve as a test of individuality, are refraction, both single and double, and polarization of light. The high refractive power of the diamond led the illustrious Newton to conclude that it was combustible, a fact verified by subsequent experiments.

Refractive power is the property all transparent substances have of altering the direction of a ray of light impinging on their surfaces.

Single refraction is where the ray is simply bent from its original course and proceeds in another direction while passing through the transparent body. When it becomes divided into two rays which proceed in different directions, it is double refraction; and the test of identity of any substance based on refraction is the refractive index of that substance, which may be explained and found as follows:

Let abcd be a closed vessel, having a small hole at e, then suppose f to be a luminous point, as a candle, the light proceeding from it would, if the vessel were empty, go in a straight line to g; but fill the vessel with water up to the level h, h, then the ray of light falling on the water at i would not as before go on to g, but would be bent or refracted, and proceed to some other point, as g'. If now a line be drawn perpendicular to the surface of the water at i, the angle f i j' is called the angle of incidence, the angle g' i j', the angle of refraction, and between these two angles, or rather their sines, a certain relation or proportion holds, which is invariable in the same substance, however much the angle of incidence may vary, and is different in different transpar-

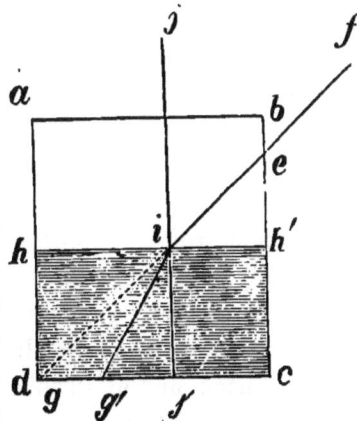

ent bodies, as water, glass, etc., etc., and that is the refractive index, and is usually indicated by the Greek letter μ thus—

$$\frac{\text{Sin. angle incidence.}}{\text{Sin. angle of refraction.}} = \mu$$

To obtain the sine of an angle let abc be an angle, and cd, a perpendicular line on one side of the angle, then the length of cd, divided by the length of cb, is called the sine of the angle abc. It may be said as a general rule the value of μ is high in proportion to the density of the substance.

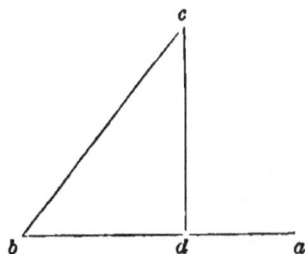

In double refraction one of the separated rays (ordinary ray) follows the law above given, the other (extraordinary ray) a different law. And the angle of separation depends on the direction in which the light is transmitted, and in all substances there is at least one line along which the ray of light suffers no separation. This line is called the axis of the crystal, or of double refraction. But the property of double refraction is difficult of investigation in ordinary cases.

Polarization of light: when a ray of light falls on a plate of transparent glass, inclined at an angle of about 56 degrees, and after reflection therefrom falls on a second plate of glass at an angle of 56 degrees, it will be found that when the second plate is horizontal the ray will be reflected from it; but when, still preserving its inclination of 56 degrees, it is turned round so as to be vertical, the ray will no longer be reflected and will disappear. The ray after incidence is said to be polarized, the test of its polarization being that it refuses to be reflected from the second plane at right angles to the plane of incidence. The angle 56 degrees, by which light becomes polarized by incidence on glass, is called the polarizing angle. This angle is different for different bodies.

Light may also be polarized by transmission through tourmaline, Iceland spar, or other double refracting bodies.

To determine the polarizing angle of a body, we have only to reflect a ray of light from its surface, at such an angle that it shall refuse to be reflected by a plate of glass inclined at an angle of 56 degrees placed in a plane at right angles to the first plane of reflection, or that it shall be incapable of transmission through a plate of tourmaline properly disposed.

The refractive index of a body may be also ascertained from the polarizing angle by the following relation :
μ = tan. polarizing angle.

Electricity can be excited in many precious stones by friction, heat, or pressure; some are conductors, some non-conductors. The faculty of the retention of electricity, and the time which elapses before they lose it, forms a distinguishing mark and test of the identity of many gems. The Abbe Haüy, in his valuable work on gems, speaks of this property at great length. The Indians of the East have long been acquainted with it, and the Greeks called amber "electron," on account of its power excited by friction of attracting small bodies.

Diaphaneity. Most gems are transparent to a greater or less degree, and their different degrees of transparency are distinguished by the following terms.

Transparent : when objects can be seen distinctly through them.

Semi-transparent: when the outlines of objects seen through them are indistinct.

Translucent : when only light is transmitted and objects are invisible.

Semi-translucent: when translucent at the edges only.

Opaque : when no light is transmitted.

Some gems are also fusible, and some not, and the ease or difficulty experienced in fusing them affords a mode of ascertaining their composition and coloring matter. The diamond is infusible although combustible ; the ruby, sapphire, etc., are fusible with borax.

Diamond. This gem surpasses all others in hardness and brilliancy; its specific gravity is about 3.5, its cleavage very perfect, its refraction simple, it is transparent, translucent, combustible, infusible, and unassailable by acids, and is composed of pure crystallized carbon. By exposure to light it frequently becomes phosphorescent, smaller ones quicker than larger; it is found in both regular crystalline forms and in an amorphous state. The crystals are generally octahedrons, or dodecahedrons, the planes of which are often concave or convex ; sometimes they are worn by attrition or other causes into heterogeneous forms of all shapes. The diamond is obtained of all colors—orange, red, white, yellow, green, blue, pink, brown, black, and opalescent. There is a slight difference in the specific gravity of the Oriental and the Brazilian diamond, and also between the white and colored. The following seems to be the result of numerous experiments:

		white 3.442
Specific gravity of Brazilian diamonds		yellow 3.520

			white 3.524
"	"	Indian or Golconda	yellow 3.566

The Indian is chiefly octahedral shaped, the Brazilian dodecahedral, and in the new fields in Africa both forms are obtained. This gem is a non-conductor of electricity, and becomes positively electric by friction, but loses its power within half an hour. It is one of those sub. stances which reflect all the light falling on the posterior surfaces at an angle of incidence greater than 24° 13'. Its power of refraction is great, and its dispersion small in comparison. For instance—

Refraction of the Diamond 2. 487
" " Glass 1. 525
Dispersion of the Diamond 0. 38
" " Glass 0. 32

Its extraordinary play and brilliancy are attributable to these qualities, and on account of them scientific men have endeavored to apply the diamond to optical and microscopical purposes. But Sir David Brewster found that the inequalities of its structure caused too much aberration of light to make it serviceable for such

9

purposes. It does not possess the power of polarizing
light, yet the same scholar gave it as his opinion, that
in some cases light was slightly changed in passing
through it.

The diamond cuts glass with great facility, but all
stones of this species cannot be used for that purpose ;
the angles must be naturally acute; they are then
called "glaziers," and are worth $50 the carat. Most
gems will scratch glass, but the diamond only is capable of cutting it. This gem is not acted upon by acids,
but it is a combustible body, becoming entirely consumed when exposed to a strong degree of heat (14°
Wedgwood). Newton, from its high refractive power,
early surmised the fact of its combustibility. But the
first record of its really having been burnt was at the
academy of Florence, under the dukedom of Cosmo III.,
in 1694. It was accomplished by means of powerful
burning glasses, the diamond first splitting, then emitting sparks, and at last disappeared, leaving no trace
behind. The Emperor Francis I. exposed diamonds
and rubies together in an assayer's furnace for twenty-
four hours, when the diamond had disappeared and the
rubies remained in their normal state. Some French
chemists also burnt a fine diamond, in the year 1771 ;
but it seemed to be still a question among the learned
whether the stones were burnt, became vaporized, or
split into impalpable powder, until a French jeweler,
named Maillard, having declared that he had frequently
exposed diamonds to heat as intense as that which had
consumed the others, without injury, and offering to
submit some to the test. He imbedded them in char-

coal dust and sealed them hermetically in a clay pipe bowl, and after leaving them in the furnace for the same time, took them out uninjured, thus clearly proving the diamond, like other combustible bodies, only really burns when in connection with the oxygen of the air. Lavoisier burnt a diamond in oxygen, and obtained the same result as arises from the combustion of pure carbon—carbonic acid. Another chemist, Clouet, made steel by exposing iron and diamond together, proving its identity with carboniferous substances, showing that it burns readily when exposed in the open air or in gas, to an intense heat, with a bright red flame, and that it gives out sparks during combustion. It may be well here to state that at a great fire in Hamburg some years ago many diamonds, which had remained in the burning buildings, were afterwards sold for trifling sums, and to an inexperienced eye appeared valueless; but when repolished regained their pristine brilliancy, though with a slight loss in weight.

This gem can be cloven with facility in a direction parallel with the planes of the octahedron or dodecahedron; in other words, "splits easily with the grain." This quality much assists the operation of cutting or grinding, especially where it is desirable to get rid of flaws. Notwithstanding its hardness it is capable of being reduced to powder, and the mistaken idea that the best test of its genuineness was to lay it on an anvil and strike it with the hammer, when, if real, it either breaks the hammer or buries itself in the anvil, has caused the loss of many fine gems, which were either crushed or thrown away as worthless.

As heretofore intimated, no person has as yet pro-
posed a theory which could account for the formation of
the stone under consideration. Nor has any one succeeded in discovering the matter which gives a color to
this gem. Liebig has declared his opinion to be that
the tinge arises from the presence of uncrystallized vegetable substance. The flaws and black specks which
so frequently appear might be supposed to arise from
imperfectly crystallized carbon, analogous to carbonate,
hereafter alluded to, but this neither has ever been satisfactorily determined. Many chemists and mineralogists have affirmed that by means of heat the natural
colors can be expelled or improved; but experience
shows this theory to be a mistake, although when the
stone is exposed to strong heat it appears whiter; yet
this is occasioned simply from a crust formed on the
outside, impairing the transparency, and after being repolished the original color returns. Still, red flaws
which have been found in the rough stone, do sometimes lose their color by exposure to great heat, and in
some instances become black.

A gentleman by the name of Barbat is said to have
discovered and employed, for the last fifteen years, a
process which, it is reported, enables him to remove
the opaque crust which covers some diamonds in the
rough state, so as to show the color they will have
when cut. This might render the work of the lapidary
more easy.

In ancient times, in India, the use of this gem was
one of the regal privileges of the Hindoo Rajahs and
Sultans, but after the overthrow of the Indian king-

doms and dynasties it was more generally worn. The finest diamond found in the possession of the Mahratta of Peshawur, at the conquest of the Deccan by the English, was called, by the East India Company, Nassak, and valued at £30,000, and is now owned by the Marquis of Westminster. The origin of the carat weight by which gems are measured, is from the Arabic word *kuara*, the name of the seeds of a pod-bearing plant growing on the gold-coast of Africa, which are invariably of an equal weight, and were first used for weighing the grains or dust of gold. It was adopted in Hindostan, and has thence spread over the whole world.

Carbonate, or diamond carbon, is a substance whose hardness is identical with the diamond, with its specific gravity 3.012 to 3.416. It sometimes takes a polish equal to diamond, and seems to be carbon imperfectly crystallized. When burned, it leaves a residue of clay and other substances. It is in some cases of a brownish-green opaque color; in others of a granular structure and porous, resembling pumice stone, dense, very massive, and found in lumps occasionally as large as a walnut. It is used in the form of powder to cut and polish diamonds and other gems. Carbonate would appear to be the connecting link between uncrystallized carbon and the diamond; and a scientific examination of it might lead to a further knowledge of the formation of that gem.

The brilliancy and beauty of the diamond is comparatively but feebly displayed in rough stones. In order to fit them for personal ornaments they require cutting

and polishing, which bring out their lustre and charms
in its true light; and, therefore, on the skill with which
this is performed—on the regularity of the facets and the
perfect polish depend the value of the gem, nearly as
much as on the original material ; for the purest stone,
cut by unskillful hands, may remain a dull mass, without life or lustre.

Lewis Van Berghem, or Berguem, has had the fame
of being the first discoverer of the art of cutting and
polishing diamonds with their own powder, in 1456,
but the original knowledge can hardly be ascribed to
him, when it is remembered that nearly a century before that time, in 137.3, the Emperor Charles had the
clasps of his cloak ornamented with these gems, and
in church decorations of even an earlier date were set
diamonds with ground edges, a table, and the lower
parts cut as a four-sided pyramid; and in an inventory
of the effects of the Duke of Anjou, made about the
year 1364, mention is made of a diamond cut in the
form of a shield.   Yet the mode of cutting, at that
early period, was rude, and added but little to the
beauty and lustre of the stone, and it was ranked less
in value than many other gems.

In 1407, a clever artificer named Herman made
some progress in this branch of industry   But in 1456,
Lewis Van Berghem, who had studied in Paris, made
known the mode of cutting the diamond into regular
facets, and this discovery made a complete revolution
in the trade, so that he was considered the parent of
the art, and a guild of cutters were established by him
in Bruges, and in 1475 he made the first trial of his

improved method upon three large stones furnished by Charles the Bold, Duke of Burgundy. The largest, the "Sancy," hereafter mentioned, the second came into the possession of Pope Sixtus IV., and the third, cut into the form of a triangle and set in a ring, was given to the faithless Louis XI. Robert Van Berghem relates that his grandfather Lewis received 3,000 ducats for cutting these stones.

The pupils of Berghem established themselves in Antwerp and Amsterdam. Cardinal Mazarin, of Paris, patronized this industry greatly; he caused the diamonds in the French crown to be recut, from which they obtained the name of the twelve Mazarins. In an inventory of the French crown jewels, made in 1774, number 349 is described as the tenth Mazarin; what has become of the rest is not known. The protection and example of the Cardinal caused a taste for these jewels to become general among the French people, and it is said that at this time there were in Paris seventy five diamond-cutters well employed. But thereafter the trade in that city declined and appears gradually to have become firmly established in Amsterdam, where it still continues one of the chief branches of industry, and where most all the diamonds are now cut.

About the end of the seventeenth century, Vincenti Peruggi, or Peruzzi, introduced, at Venice, the so-called double cutting "Brilliants recoupés." Some years ago there were several cutters in England known for the excellence of their work, and stones cut by them now bring a large price in that country, but the trade is, at the present time, nearly extinct in England. Numbers of diamonds are still cut in India, but the work is considered to be very defective, as the natives, with the view of enhancing the value of their gems, leave them as heavy as possible, after preserving the natural shape of the rough stone, and setting aside one of the first rules of cutting, that over as well as under weight detracts from the value, and that a diamond weighing seven carats with only the spread of five carats has only the value of a five carat stone.

In Amsterdam this trade is carried to its highest state of perfection, and furnishes employment to several thousand persons, mostly Jews. The largest mills are those of Mr. Coster, employing from 500 to 600 workmen. To this establishment several of the most celebrated stones have been entrusted.

The operation of cutting is commenced by taking two diamonds which it is desired to cut, and fastening each firmly into the end of a stick, with cement, leaving a part to be cut exposed; the workman then, with leather gloves on his hands, takes a stick in each, and placing the ends containing the stones together against two upright pieces of iron secured to the edge of the cutting bench, rubs the two diamonds together until he has produced a flat even surface (called a facet) in place of the concave or convex form of the natural stone, and thus a facet is cut on two stones at the same time. The powder or dust which falls is received in a box containing oil and is burnt before being used, to free it from the particles of cement or other matter that may have fallen into it. During the operation the facets are examined, first removing the powder with a camel's hair pencil, then moistening the stone with the tongue. When one facet is formed, the cement is heated and the diamond taken out, inserted again so as to expose a different surface on which to cut another face, and so on until the cutting is completed. By this means, only the general outline of the form is made. A stone which would have, when completed, fifty-eight facets, would receive in cutting only eighteen; eight being the surface of an octahedron or double pyramid, and the eighteen being formed by taking away the eight edges or angles of these eight surfaces, with one for the whole table and one for the culet. In polishing, the remaining facets are formed and the lustre produced. This is done with diamond powder on a steel disk or "skaif," which is made to revolve with great velocity by steam or horse power. The skaif is prepared by first rubbing its surface with an ordinary whet stone in such a direction as to form tangents of a circle, whose diameter is about one-third that of the skaif; thus are formed deep scratches or indented lines on its whole surface, after which it is rubbed with a fine hone or turkey stone in the direction of the diameter, until the former marks are nearly effaced; by the crossing of the scratches a soft grain is formed which will retain the diamond powder. This is then spread on the prepared steel with olive oil and the flat surface of a finished diamond held against it while in motion to force the powder into the wheel. The stone to be polished is then inserted into melted solder in the hollow top of a brass-handled stick, and by allowing the solder to cool, becomes fixed

9 *

in its proper position. The polishing is then performed and the additional facets made by holding it against the powder on the revolving skaif, the solder being melted and the position of the stone changed as often as necessary; the process in this manner is completed. The work demands the greatest accuracy, the least inattention or irregularity may spoil the beauty of the gem. Some of the diamonds cut and polished in this way are so small that a thousand of them will only weigh one carat, and when the minuteness of the facets required on such a stone is considered, it will be readily understood that the labor requires workmen of the highest skill.

Diamonds not fit for double cutting and the splinters from them are made into single cut, the rest are formed into brilliants or roses.

The most experienced judges cannot always determine with certainty what a stone will be when polished. Flaws and imperfections are often laid bare, which go deeper than the appearance of the rough gem would lead them to predict, and also the color seen in a rough diamond is sometimes found to arise from the presence of flaws or specks which are removed in cutting, thus leaving the stone white.

Diamond crushing is performed by placing the boart in a steel mortar, fitted with an air-tight pestle, with which it is reduced to splinters; it is then placed with olive oil into another hardened steel mortar with a pestle of hardened steel, where it is crushed to an impalpable powder, which, when burnt to remove the oil, is of a grey color.

Diamond splitting or cleavage has a double purpose,

the renewal, of defective parts and the formation of facets in the rough.   But it is only applied when the natural form of the stone would require great time and labor in cutting in the regular way, and on account of its shape ; the process is greatly shortened by splitting, and at the same time " usable " pieces may be split off. To perform this operation, the diamond is fastened in the end of a stick, with cement, as heretofore stated, leaving the part to be split off exposed.   In order to avoid missing the proper plane of cleavage, a line is scratched on the surface to mark the exact place, first with a complete crystal, then with a sharp splinter to deepen the impression, and lastly, with a very fine splinter, to make a very deep mark ; the cement stick then being placed in a piece of lead fastened to the workman's bench, a very fine knife is inserted in the mark, and by a smart blow with the hammer, the gem is split.

Stones difficult to split are sawn with fine iron wires, fitted in the saw bow and anointed with diamond powder and olive oil.   Likewise larger stones, where the risk of splitting is too great, or where the direction of natural cleavage would reduce the size too much, are sawn.

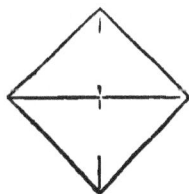

Side view of Rough Diamond.   Side view of Diamond partially cut.   Side view of double cut Diamond.

The above cuts are intended to represent, first, a dia·
mond in its natural state; second, when the upper and
under facets, called respectively the table and culet,
are formed ; and third, when fully cut, the broadest part
or edge is called the girdle. The space from the table
to the girdle, is named the bezil or bizil ; that from the
girdle to the culet, the pavilion. The facets on the
bezel touching the table only, and forming triangles, are
called star facets ; those touching the girdle, skill facets;
and the others, the lozenge-shaped facets, touching both
table and girdle. The triangular facets on the pavilion,
touching the girdle, are under skill facets, etc., etc.
The culet is square or octagonal.

Double cut brilliants are the most common form at
the present day. The shape of the rough diamond is
generally that of two pyramids joined at the base; if
not, it must be made so by art; then to produce the table, five-eighteenths of the total thickness are taken
away from one pyramid, and for the culet, one-
eighteenth from the other. The proportions of the
cut stone are as follows : From the table to the girdle,
one-third ; and from the girdle to the culet, two-thirds
of the total thickness. The diameter of the table four-
ninths of that of the girdle, the diameter of the culet
one-fifth of that of the table. The girdle should be of
the same dimensions as the thickness or depth ; the
triangular facets on the under side, from the culet to
the girdle, half as deep again as the upper star facets,
and a diamond well cut will have a thin edge at the
girdle.

The single cut brilliant, the old form of cutting, has

only thirty-eight facets, and the table is square ; there are sixteen triangular facets touching it and the girdle ; the pavilion has twelve touching the girdle, and under them eight long facets.

Some old single cut stones have the table cut in the form of a star. And there are some old gems dismounted from ornaments brought from India, having only a table culet, and eight, or perhaps sixteen, facets, and are called table diamonds.

In the rose-cut diamond, instead of a pointed culet, the under part is quite flat, and the upper terminates in a point. The work consists of triangles, whose apices meet at the point, below which is another row reversed so as together to form lozenges, and the apices of the under triangle touch the girdle, leaving spaces which are each cut into two facets.

The rules for the dimensions of a well proportioned rose are : the depth, half the diameter of the under side ; the diameter of the crown, three-fifths of the base ; and the perpendicular, from the base to the crown, three-fifths of the depth of the stone. The round stones are best adapted for this mode of cutting. Roses are often cut drop-shaped, oval, or any form which the rough stone admits, with the least waste of material, and frequently with less facets, as those called Antwerp roses.

Rose diamonds at one time became unfashionable and were superseded by brilliants. But many persons are now wearing them. The same amount of display is secured at much less cost. A very beautiful form in the last mentioned mode of cutting, particularly for pen-

deloques, is called the brilliotte or briolet, shaped like two rose diamonds joined at the base, but it is very rarely seen.

In conclusion, of the subject of cutting it may be said that the process of cutting colored stones and other gems is so much like that of diamonds, except the different shapes and substances with which the cutting is performed, that it is hardly worth while to spend further time on that point, especially as this work is not intended to be a lexicon for the jeweler or merchant, but simply a general treatise for the public, and, therefore, nothing further will be said of this art, and we will proceed with the properties of gems.

The ruby, or red sapphire, is the most valuable of all gems when of large size and perfect, exceeding even the diamond in value. Its hardness is superior to any known substance except the diamond, being numbered nine in Moh's scale; its specific gravity is 3·9 to 4·1; it is susceptible of electricity by friction; its component parts are:

Alumina . . . . 98·5
Oxide of Iron . . . . 1·0
Lime. . . . . 0·5

The coloring arises from metallic oxides, chrome, etc.

The ruby, like all other corundums, is infusible alone, but melts with difficulty in combination with a flux into clear glass. Its refraction is double. The system of crystallization to which it belongs is rhombohedral; the cleavage basal—that is, the crystal breaks across the prisms with a flat surface; its lustre is vitreous. The

color varies from the lightest rose tint to the deepest
carmine; the very light or very dark are not so highly
esteemed. The most valuable is that shade called the
"pigeon's-blood," a pure, deep, rich red, without any
admixture of colors. Sometimes specimens of this gem
are obtained asteriated, or with a star in the direction
of the axis, the points of which terminate at the plane
of the hexagonal prism, in a section across it. They
are called star rubies, the star appearing to be formed
by a silky imperfection in the gem, which shows forth
with great distinctness when examined by the light of a
candle or of the sun. When the stone has a fine colors
the asteriation adds greatly to its beauty and value,
care being taken in cutting to get the centre of the star
in the middle of the gem. This variety has always been
greatly prized in the eastern countries. Brahmin traditions speak of the abode of the gods lighted by enor-.
mous rubies. In China these gems have long been
used for ornamenting the slippers of women, and many
of them are met with there as in India.

Rubies are spoken of in the Bible, in Proverbs and
the book of Job; and there can hardly be a doubt that
they were well known to the ancient Greeks and Romans. The Indian carbuncle mentioned by Pliny, and
the anthrax of Theophrastus were doubtless rubies;
these authors ascribed to it the power of giving light in
the dark. Ancient cameos and intaglios are still in existence, engraved on this stone five hundred years before
Christ, which, it is well known, was the period when
art was carried to its highest perfection in Greece.
Pliny also speaks of the Ethiopians increasing the splen-

dor of rubies by laying them for fourteen days in vinegar, which added to their lustre for a time, after which they became softer and more brittle.

In later times it was thought to be an amulet against poison, plague, sadness, evil thoughts, etc., and kept the wearer in health, and cheered his mind; and if the donor was in danger, it was supposed to become black or obscure, and would not resume its color till the danger had passed away.

There are but very few large rubies of fine quality in existence: one in the French crown jewels, cut in the form of a dragon with extended wings, adorns the order of the Golden Fleece. Tavernier, in the account of his travels, speaks of one in possession of the king of Vishapoor, of fine quality, weighing fifty carats. It is said the king of Burmah has one as large as a pigeon's egg, of extraordinary quality. There is one in the Russian treasury of large size, and among the crown jewels of Austria are several of considerable size.

Interesting experiments have of late been made by chemists, in forming by artificial means minute crystals of a red color, of the same form of crystallization as, and of equal hardness to, the natural ruby, but those produced are very minute, and as small rubies are plentiful, it is doubtful whether the experiment or expense of manufacturing will ever prove remunerative. They are made by heating alumina for a long time with borax in a vessel of platinum: the borax first dissolves the alumina, and then the elements of the borax separate and disappear by volatilization, leaving the alumina in a crystallized state.

Colored crystals of alumina have also been formed by bringing gas, fluoride of silicon, in contact with the vapor of boracic acid, at a high temperature, when mutual decomposition takes place; fluoride of boron escapes, and the alumina is left distinctly crystallized. It is a curious fact, that the same matter under identically similar circumstances communicates sometimes a red, and at others a blue, color, which corresponds with the conditions in which both rubies and sapphires are found in nature, both blue (sapphire), and red (ruby), crystals occurring together.

Sapphire, as heretofore stated, is identical with the ruby, differing only in color, on account of which it bears another name. It is composed of the same materials, in the same proportions. It possesses the same hardness, electrical and other properties. Its color varies from white to the deepest b'ue or black; it seldom has a pure blue throughout; occasionally black is intermixed, giving an inky hue; sometimes red, perceptible only by candle light, bringing out an amethystine tint. Sapphires, presenting the same hue by daylight, may differ much in color by candle-light. Often in these gems partially colored dark, there is a way of cutting by which all the dark portion is taken off, except a small spot reserved for the culet, leaving the upper part perfectly white, but when looked at from the table presents a most vivid blue shade, often superior to that of stones colored throughout. The parts colored and uncolored can be distinctly seen by holding the stone, with a pair of forceps, an inch beneath the surface of clear water. This applies to all gems. There is, also, an asteriated variety of this gem, usually of a grayish-blue tint, called star sapphires. The white sapphire resembles the diamond so well, that when cut and polished they have been sold to persons conversant with the trade as diamonds. But the difference can be at once ascertained by taking the specific gravity or testing the hardness.

The most valuable sapphires are considered to be those which approximate in color to the blue velvet of the shade formerly called "bleu du roi," and should appear blue by candle-light as well as by day. The name sapphire is found in all languages, with but slight alteration. The Hebrew (סַפִּיר), sapphir; Chaldaic, sapirinon; Greek, zappiros; Latin, sapphirus, etc. But the ancients applied the name to all stones of blue color, without distinction. Pliny, Theophrastus, Aristotle, and others, speaking of blue stones spotted or veined with gold (probably lapis-lazuli), call them sapphirus, although they were acquainted with the true oriental sapphire. Isidorus remarks: "Sapphirus cœruleus est cum purpura, habens pulveres aureos sparsos," the particles of pyrites sometimes found in lapis lazuli having the appearance of gold specks.

Pliny, speaking of the same stone, in his beautiful style says: "In sapphiris aurum punctis collucet cœrulis; similis est cœlo sereno, propter aurea puncta stellis ornato." "In the blue sapphire shine golden specks; it is like the serene sky adorned with stars, on account of the golden points." The ancients also called sapphires male or female, according to the color—the pale blue, approaching the white, female; and the deep colored or indigo, male.

This gem was sacred to Apollo, and was worn when inquiring of the oracle at his shrine. The magical properties ascribed to it were, that it prevents evil and impure thoughts; that it is an enemy to poison, and if put in a glass with a venomous reptile it will kill it. St. Jerome, in his exposition of the 19th chapter of Isaiah, asserts that it procures favor with princes, pacifies enemies, obtains freedom from captivity, and frees from enchantments. Boetius states, that on account of its attachment to chastity it was worn by priests; and Galen and Dioscorides speaks of its medical properties. It was supposed to be a remedy against fevers.

In the treasuries and regalias of Europe are many sapphires, and some of great size. In the Vienna Keoneuschätze is said to be one of marvellous beauty and size. The green vaults at Dresden contain several remarkable for these qualities. · In the Russian treasury, also, there are some of large size. There are some of considerable value, size and beauty owned by private individua's.

There are other varieties of corundum met with, such as Oriental amethyst, topaz, emerald, aquamarine, etc., named from their color; but they are mostly of rare occurrence, and generally pass for, or are confounded with, the gems whose name they bear, but may usually be distinguished from them by their superior hardness, play, brilliancy, and specific gravity.

CHAPTER XII.

CHRYSOBERYL, cymophane, and cat's-eye, are different names applied to one variety of a brilliant gem of yellow color; some with a greenish or brownish shade, and occasionally white; some showing a reddish tint by transmitted light; some possess an opalescence, and when cut "en cabochon" are called crysolite, crysoberyl, cat's-eye, or cymophanes. The properties of this stone are, specific gravity from 3.680 to 3.754, varying; its hardness in the scale is numbered as 8.5; being scratched by ruby, sapphire, etc., and scratching quartz; it acquires electricity by friction, retaining it several hours; it possesses double refraction; its lustre is vitreous; its system of crystallization is trimetric or rhombic; it varies from being transparent to nearly opaque; its cleavage is not perfect, and it breaks with a conchoidal fracture, rather uneven; it is infusible alone before the blow-pipe, but with borax or salt of phosphorus melts with difficulty to a clear glass; it is unaffected by acids; it is composed of

Alumina.............. ....80.2
Glucina.........................19.8

with traces of protoxide of iron, copper, and oxide of lead, according to color and locality in which it is found.

Those semi-transparent are called cymophane, and are the cat's-eye of commerce. The variety used in jewelry are yellow and transparent, and when cut in brilliant form are extremely lively and lustrous, very much resembling yellow diamonds. They are not fashionable, however, and are rarely mounted as ornaments. These stones are sometimes called, and mistaken for, crysolites, but the error can be easily detected, the hardness and specific gravity being so dissimilar. They can also be distinguished from the yellow topaz, as they do not become electric by heat, a property of that stone.

The ancients seem to have confounded this gem with crysolite, and it appears, also, to have been a stone of a different quality, possibly the crysoprase. Crysoberyl is cut on a copper wheel with emery, and polished with tripoli. The value of the transparent is quite nominal, but the cymophane or crysoberyl (cat's-eye) is more marketable. They are considered lucky, and instances are known of cat's-eyes of great size and beauty bringing extravagant prices. An English nobleman, not long since, paid fully £1,000 for one, but such value is purely an illusion.

The emerald and beryl are stones of the same composition, like the ruby and sapphire, differing only in colors; the emerald is a beautiful green, whilst the beryl or aquamarine is a light blue or sea green. These gems form beautiful specimens for the student of mineralogy, the rich green of the emerald contrasting strongly with the lime-stone matrix in which it is found imbedded, and the beryl is obtained in crystals of great size and many shades of color, and sometimes transparent. Their properties are, hardness from 7.5 to 8 Moh's scale; cleavage, imperfectly basal; specific gravity 2.67 to 2.75, the weight of sapphire being nearly double that of emerald; it is unaffected by acids, but is soluble with salt of phosphorus (microsmic salt); the lustre is vitreous, rarely resinous. These stones are very brittle; emerald when first taken from the mine is so soft as to crumble by friction, but hardens by exposure.

Their compositions are:

	Emerald.	Beryl.
Silica	68.50....	.........67.00
Alumina	15.75..............	...16.50
Glucina	12.50......	.......14.50
Peroxide of iron	1.00....	.... 1.00
Lime	0.25..........	... 0.50
Oxide of chrome	0.30...........	.. ——
Magnesia, lime and soda traces.		

What constitutes the coloring matter in these stones has not been satisfactorily explained. Pliny, in speaking of the emerald, says, that in the island of Cyprus, on the tomb of Hermias, was sculptured a lion with eyes of emerald which shone so brightly as to frighten away the fish; but the fishermen, having these gems removed and replaced by others less brilliant, the fish again returned to their accustomed haunts.

Nero observed the feats of the gladiators through an eye-glass of emerald. Isidorus says it surpasses any green herb or plant in color, and gives a green shade to the surrounding air. It was used in the middle ages in church cups and chalices, and Charlemagne had a lustrous emerald in his crown.   Vast quantities of this gem were obtained from Peru at its conquest.   It is said Cortez presented a hundred-weight to the king of Spain, besides giving to his bride several emeralds carved in various forms, and one very large, shaped like a rose—a gift which aroused the envy of the queen and caused him to lose his favor at court.

Necklaces of this gem have been found in Etruscan tombs and at Herculaneum.   The ancients dedicated it to Mercury, and ascribed to it the following properties : It was considered good for the eyes, and on that account worn as a seal ring ; it was supposed to color water, in which it was placed, green ; to preserve chastity ; and ground into powder and taken as a remedy for various diseases.   The orientals, even now, believe it imparts courage and averts the plague.

It ranks in value next the ruby and is a favorite gem.   The treasuries of Europe and Asia are rich in this jewel ; the low price which it formerly brought and its pleasing color having caused it to be collected and worn in every country.   There is said to be one in Austria weighing 2,000 carats, and the Duke of Devonshire, England, has one weighing nearly nine ounces.   The value of the beryl, on the other hand, is trifling, and is not much used, except for imitation-jewelry and orna- ments for metal work.   It was known to the Romans, and Pliny mentions it as the gem green as the sea, "Qui viriditate puri maris imitantur," hence it is called "aquamarine."   Beads of beryl have been found in the mummy pits of Egypt, and the Greeks used it for intaglios over two thousand years ago.

Spinel and balas ruby are also identically the same gem, spinel being supposed to be, or applied to, the deeper hued, which has a fine lively red color, but with a cinnamon tint, rendering it less brilliant than the true ruby or red sapphire.

It belongs to the cubic system of crystallization, and is found in octahedral crystals; its lustre is vitreous; it is transparent in various degrees, sometimes nearly opaque; it is of great hardness and numbered 8 in the scale; it has not the property of acquiring electricity either by heat or friction; it is infusible before the blowpipe and possesses simple refraction; it is composed of:

Alumina	69.01
Magnesia	26.21
Protoxide of iron	0.71
Oxide of Chrome	1.10
Silica	2.02

The spinel and balas ruby are of very similar composition; the other varieties differ in the proportion of their constituents; and some possess an admixture of other substances. Red spinel, on being heated, becomes brown, and as it cools becomes first more opaque, then green, then almost colorless, and finally resumes its pristine hue. The balas ruby is of a lighter or rose pink color. A true ruby can be easily distinguished from these stones by the hardness and specific gravity. The same supernatural powers have been attributed to these gems as to the true ruby; its value is very uncertain and variable.

Topaz is a gem not in vogue at the present time for

the purpose of jewelry. The true topaz seldom occurs of a large size without defects; it is obtained of many colors and is given different names for different colors, as follows: The colorless is called nova mina; the light blue Brazilian, sapphire; the greenish, aquamarine; greenish yellow, Brazilian crysolite; the artificially obtained, pink or rose color, Brazilian ruby. Its system of crystallization is trimetric; its cleavage, basal; its specific gravity, 3.5 to 3.6; it is numbered 8 in the scale of hardness; possesses double refraction in a slight degree; its lustre is vitreous and its composition is:

	Brazilian Topaz.	Saxon Topaz.
Silica	34.01	34.24
Alumina	58.38	57.45
Fluorine	15.06	14.99

Monsieur St. Clair Deville has detected Vanadium in the variety from Brazil. Crystals of this stone are usually hemihedral (half form), that is, its angles are removed from the original form, to wit: the hemihedral form of the cube is the tetrahedron. It becomes strongly electric by heat, friction, and pressure, and retaining it for several hours; it is infusible on charcoal, but with very strong heat blisters are formed; it fuses with borax into a clear glass and becomes blue with cobalt solution. If sulphuric acid be applied to this gem, it yields hydrofluori; but muriatic does not affect it. The crystals are not usually large, seldom exceeding two or three inches in length, and are mostly well defined. There is found in Brazil, associated with the topaz, a very rare mineral called enclase, of a pale blue or green color, quite like aquamarine.

10

A large mass of white topaz, now in one of the cases of the British museum, London, was, many years ago, used as a door weight by a marine store dealer, in that city, who sold it for three shillings. It weighs twelve pounds.

Topaz, no doubt, was known in very early times; it is mentioned in the Bible, and there are in existence intaglios formed of this stone, of early Greek workmanship. The large, so-called, diamond in the Portuguese treasury, is supposed to be a white topaz—it is larger than a hen's egg and weighs 1,680 carats. The ancients ascribed to topaz the following properties: Discovering poison by becoming obscured when in contact with it; it quenched the heat of boiling water; it calmed the passions; prevented bad dreams; and its power increased and decreased with the full or wane of the moon. The Emperor Hadrian is said to have had a topaz seal ring, engraved with these lines:

> Natura deficit,
> Fortuna mutatur,
> Deus omnia cernit.

And Pliny mentions topaz as being found in the mines of alabaster, near the city of Thebes.

The zircon, hyacinth or jacinth, is a gem of various colors, red, yellow, green, brown, grey, white; it is of the diametric system of crystallization, and is very imperfectly cleavable; its specific gravity of 4.07 to 4.75, with a lustre nearly adamantine, but in the opaque variety it is vitreous; its fracture is conchoidal and brilliant; it is unaffected by acids, except sulphuric; it is infusible alone, and melts with borax into transparent

glass. It is made phosphorescent by heat, at the same
time loses its color and increases in specific gravity; but
the second time heated, the phosphorescence does not
appear. It is composed of

Zirconia 66.8
Silica.......................... 33.2
Peroxide of Iron................ 0.1

It is seldom used for jewelry, yet a solitary specimen
free from defects, of fine color, may bring a high price.
When of a greyish or smoky white, it is called a jargoon, and is often sold for diamond, which its lustre resembles. In the last century, jargoon was supposed to
be an inferior diamond, and was much used in mourning ornaments; it possesses the power of double refraction to a high degree, but is rarely perfectly transparent. Zircon was well known to the ancients, but it
is doubtful whether the stone they gave the name was
the same as the stone which at present bears it. Its
supposed magical properties were; it procured sleep,
riches, honor, and wisdom, and drove away plague and
evil spirits.

Tourmaline is of many varieties and colors, red and
pink, called rubelite; blue, called indicalite; white,
brown, and black—the only kind used in jewelry being of a dark olive green tint. Its crystallization is hexagonal or rhombohedral; its cleavage difficult; the fracture imperfectly conchoidal; its hardness 7.0 to 7.5; specific gravity 2.99 to 3.33; lustre, vitreous; it is of all
grades of diaphaneity, from transparent to opaque; its
refraction double; its powers of polarizing light are

great, and cut into slices it is used in the polariscope for analyzing the optical properties of other minerals. It is sometimes found in a massive state ; it acquires electricity by heat or friction.

The composition of some of the different varieties is as follows—analysis by Rammelsberg :

	Black variety from Greenland.	Green variety from Brazil.	Red variety from Siberia.
Silica,	37.70	39.16	38.38
Boracic Acid,	7.36	4.59	7.41
Alumina,	34.53	40.00	43.97
Peroxide of Iron,	4.63	....	....
Protoxide of Iron,	0.25	5.96	....
Magnesia,	9.51	....	1.60
Lime,	1.25	....	0.62
Soda,	2.00	....	1.97
Potash,	0.43	3.59	0.21
Phosphorus,	0.11	....	0.27
Fluorine,	2.23	...	2.47
Peroxide of Mangonese,	....	2.14	2.60
Loss by Ignition,	...	1.58	....
Lithia,	....	....	0.48

The tourmaline has very little commercial value except for optical purposes.

The garnet is a gem much used in jewelry, its abundance rendering it of little value, while it has every quality necessary for ornamental purposes. There are many varieties and colors—red, yellow, white, black, green, brown, etc. Its hardness varies from 6.5 to 7.5 ; its specific gravity from 3.5 to 4.3 : its lustre vitreous, sometimes resinous, as in calophonite. It belongs to the monometric, or cubic system of crystallization, and is obtained in rhombic dodecahedral crystals, also massive and in small pebbles; its cleavage is dodecahe-

dral when found in a matrix. Its diaphaneity varies
from transparent to subtranslucent or nearly opaque,
and its fracture is uneven; it becomes electric by friction, and affects the magnetic needle. The kinds used
in jewelry are called carbuncle, cinnamon-stone,
(essonite), pyrope or Bohemian, besides the leucite,
melanite, colophonite, grossularite, and uwarowite which
are only interesting to the student of mineralogy. The
chemical composition of the several varieties differs.
The common garnet is essentially a silicate of alumina
iron. The others are divided according to their bases
as follows: Alumina lime garnet, alumina iron garnet,
alumina magnesia garnet, alumina manganese garnet,
iron lime garnet, lime chrome garnet.

The composition of the most important is as follows,
to-wit :

	Essonite.	Almandine.	Pyrope.
Silica,..................	38.80	36.30	40.00
Alumina.................	21.20	20.50	28.50
Protoxide of Iron,.......	....	43.20	....
Peroxide of Iron,.......	....	....	16.50
Peroxide of Manganese,..	....	....	0.25
Oxide of chrome,........	....	....	2.00
Magnesia,..............	....	....	10.00
Lime,............	27.20	....	3.50

The almandine and common garnet fuse readily,
forming glass of different colors ; but the pyrope, with
difficulty, to a black glass, while both are imperfectly
soluble in hydrochloric acid. The Syrian garnets bear
that name, not because they come from Syria, but after
Syrian, the capital of Pegu. Their color ranges from
the deepest crimson to a violet purple, resembling the

oriental amethyst. The term carbuncle is applied in-discriminately, when these gems are cut en cabochon, that is not in facets, but with a flat or hollow base and a smooth convex top. The ancients were acquainted with this stone, by the name carbuncle. Pliny describes vessels of the capacity of a pint, formed of carbuncle devoid of lustre or beauty, doubtless of the massive variety. Theophrastus mentions a Massilian carbuncle, which, held before the sun, resembled a glowing coal. The writers of the middle ages ascribed great value to it; the magical properties attributed to it were similar to those of the ruby.

The term quartz includes a large number of gems, generally of small value, although a fine specimen may bring a large price. Different colored quartz have different names, although the composition and chief characteristics are the same. Its specific gravity from 2.5 to 2.8; hardness 7; lustre vitreous when transparent, inclining to resinous when opaque; its fracture conchoidal, and its cleavage very indistinct. It possesses the power of double refraction, and becomes electric by friction; its composition is pure silica, or

Silicon.........................48.04
Oxygen................. ....51.96

It is insoluble by acids except hydrofluoric; it melts when exposed to the flame of the oxyhydrogen jet, so it can be drawn into fine threads, and at last becomes volatilized. When two pieces are rubbed together they become phosphorescent, emitting an empyreumatic odor. Its system of crystallization is rhombohedral;

some varieties massive and compact; it is found in hexagonal prisms, often with pyramids at each end. The
first variety of vitreous quartz is colorless, and called
rock-crystal; it is sometimes obtained of a very large
size, rarely perfect, however. There was a specimen in
the Jardin des Plantes, at Paris, measuring three feet in
diameter, weighing eight hundred pounds. Under the
name of pebbles, this stone is used by opticians for making the lenses of spectacles on account of its superior
hardness and durability to glass, and its coldness, as it
feels cool to the touch like all precious stones; it is also
used in the polariscope. Of late it has been used in jewelry, incrusted with stones and enamel. In India the natives hollow it out into cups, vases, and goblets, and
cover them with ornamentation.

The Chinese also use it largely, and attach great value
to it; the Japanese use it in large round balls to cool
the hands. It is sometimes made into beads for necklaces. Nero is said to have possessed two magnificent
crystal cups engraved with subjects from the Iliad at
great cost, and at his downfall he destroyed them, that
no one else might drink out of them. Many specimens
of the Cinque Cento period are still extant. Large
round balls were supposed to possess magical powers;
it was also used medicinally in powder mixed with
wine; pieces were held on the tongue in fevers to assuage thirst. In 1791 there were among the crown
treasures of France many pieces of crystal in goblets,
urns, vases, etc., some polished, and some beautifully
carved and engraved. The collection was then valued

at upwards of 1,000,000 francs. Green, pink, and other colored beads are made of crystal by artificial means.

Amethyst is quartz of a fine violet color, from white to deep purple. It is found in pieces of considerable size, and from its beautiful color and play is much used in jewelry. It takes a fine polish, and appears to the greatest advantage set with pearls or diamonds. In 1652 an amethyst was worth as much as a diamond of equal weight. In the middle ages it was believed to dispel sleep, sharpen the intellect, and to be an antidote against poison. In ancient times it was supposed to have the power of dissipating drunkenness.

Cairngorm is a variety of quartz which takes its name from the Cairngorm Mountains, Scotland, where it is obtained; it is likewise called cinnamon-stone, false topaz, etc. It has all shades of color, from yellow to black. It is found in all parts of the world, and is not much used in jewelry, except in Scotland, where it adorns the handles of snuff-mulls, dirks, powder-horns, and other articles of Highland costume.

Avanturine, or aventurine, is quartz of a brown, reddish-brown, or pearly-grey color, contains minute spangles of mica, which give it a glistening appearance. Artificial aventurine is made far more beautiful than the real. The Emperor of Russia had two large vases cut out of this material, which he presented to Sir Roderick Murchison.

Chrysoprase is of the chalcedonic variety of quartz, is massive in thick layers, which are not crystallized,

and is of a fine splintery or flat conchoidal fracture ; its
hardness is a little less than the other descriptions, and
an analysis by Klaproth gave—

Silica............................96.16
Oxide of Nickel.................. 1.00
Lime........................... 0.83

It was used by the Greeks and Romans for rings,
intaglios ; and cameos are still in existence of an early
Greek period. It is found in Kosemuty, and the kings
of Prussia used only to allow the mines to be opened
once in three years and kept the finest specimens them·
selves. Now it is of very little value.

Onyx and sardonyx are the most important of the
chalcedonic family of quartz: the onyx of a blackish or
brownish color, striped with white, sometimes with a
greenish layer. The sardonyx of deep rich brown, in
clining to orange, held before the light, shows a deep red
hue. The finest are obtained in India ; they can be
stained to any color by artificial means without difficulty.
Onyx and sardonyx are both used in jewelry, the differ·
ent layers affording good contrast for the display of en·
graving. They are also cut ·into cups, vases, knife and
sword handles, and are much used in beads for necklaces. They were used for cameos at a very early
date. In the library of the Vatican, at Rome, is the
renowned cameo said to have belonged to the Emperor
Augustus. In the imperial library, at Paris, are the
well-known onyx cameos of Marcus Aurelius and
Faustina, Agrippina and her two children, Venus rising
from the sea surrounded with cupids, and others. The
10 *

precious ring thrown into the sea by the tyrant of Samos, Polycrates, was a sardonyx.

The chaplets, or rosaries, worn by the fakirs of India, from the time of Pliny down to the present day, were, and are usually, made of onyx beads. Mithridates, king of Pontus, is reported to have had two thousand cups made of this material. This stone was supposed to cause strife and melancholy, and to cure epileptic fits.

The sard and cornelian are a variety of chalcedony, of bright red and yellow tints: the brownish-red being called sard; the bright red, white; and yellow, cornelian. They take a very beautiful polish, and are particularly adapted for seals, as they deliver easily from heated wax without destroying the impression; this quality was remarked by Pliny, who extolled the stone above the sapphire.

Chalcedony is a variety of quartz with opal disseminated through it, usually of a greyish color, sometimes milky-white, pinkish, or smalt blue—in the latter case it is called sapphire. Some Indian varieties are yellowish, owing to the presence of oxide of iron. It is not found crystallized; it is semi-transparent, translucent (to nearly opaque), with little or no lustre; it is well adapted for engraving, and has been used for that purpose from the most ancient period. White chalcedony, with minute blood-red spots, is called St. Stephen's stone.

Chalcedonyx is chalcedony having alternate stripes of white and grey. Plasma is faintly translucent, much used in olden times for engraving, and many gems of it are still extant; it is of a grass or olive green, sprinkled with yellow and white specks, with a resinous lustre.

It is found among the ruins of Rome, in the Schwarz-wald, in India and China.

Mocha, or moko, stone is a variety containing infil-trated, dendritic oxides of manganese and iron, which gives it the appearance of containing vegetable re-mains.

Agate is of many colors, usually in bands of varied thickness, sometimes the lines are zig-zag, at others nearly straight, etc. It is manufactured into articles of utility as well as ornaments. It is found in great quan-tities, and is carried as ballast in ships with light car-goes coming from Brazil, India, Australia, etc.

Cat's-eye, another chalcedonic variety of quartz, is yellowish, green yellowish, brown, blackish, or hyacinth red color: its name is derived from its opalescent lustre—held towards the light resembling the contracted purple of the eye of the cat. It is frequently confound-ed with the true or chrysoberyl cat's-eye, which is a much more beautiful gem, and can be easily distinguished by its superior hardness and greater specific gravity. The cat's-eye is much used in jewelry for rings and pins, usually set with a black or gold foile, to heighten its play and brilliancy. This stone was dedicated to the god Belus by the ancient Assyrians, and called by the classic authors *oculus Beli.*

Jasper is a variety of quartz also of various colors, dark green, yellow, red, brown, greyish, bluoish, black, and sometimes banded in stripes. It is compact, hard, and takes a good polish. The ancients prize this stone highly. Onomakritos, 500 years before Christ, speaks of "the green jasper, which rejoices the eye of man, and is looked on with pleasure by the immortals." The emeralds of the Greek and Roman authors were probably green jasper, as we have heretofore stated. In the collection of the Vatican are two marvellous vases of this substance : one of red jasper with white stripes, the other of black with yellow stripes. It is greatly prized in China, the seal of the emperor being made of it.

Bloodstone, or heliotrope, is a jasper variety of quartz of dark green with minute blood-red specks disseminated throughout. It is translucent, and susceptible of a good polish. It is used for the same purposes as agate and onyx. The word heliotrope, from two Greek words ἥλιος and τροπή signifying turning the sun, was given it from the notion that when immersed in water it changed the image of the sun into blood-red. Pliny says the sun could be viewed in it as in a mirror, and that it made visible its eclipses. Marbodus, in his poem on precious stones, affirms —

> " Ex re nomen habens est heliotropea gemma,
> Quae solis radiis in aqua subjecto basillo,
> Sanguine reddit mutato lumino solum
> Eclipsemquo novam terris effundere coget."

There is a tradition that at the crucifixion the blood which followed the spear-thrust fell upon a dark-green jasper lying at the foot of the cross, and hence the va-riety. In the middle ages the red specks were supposed to represent the blood of Christ.

The gem called chrysolite, peridot or olivine, accord-ing to color, is the true chrysolite, though not acknow-ledged as such by jewelers, who confine that name to the chrysoberyl. It belongs to the monetric system of

crystallization ; it is the softest of all gems, numbered
from 6 to 7 ; its specific gravity is 3.33 to 3.5 ; its lustre vitreous, and fracture conchoidal ; it is infusible
except that called hyolosiderite, and is easily dissolved
by sulphuric acid. It is composed of

Silica. 39.73
Magnesia 50.13
Protoxide of Iron. 9.19
Alumina. 0.32
    Protoxide of Magnesia. 0.09
Oxide of Nickel. 0.22

The deep olive-green is called peridot ; the yellowish
green, olivine ; and chrysolite when lighter or of a
greenish yellow color.   There are many other
varieties interesting only to mineralogists.   This
gem is not much used in jewelry, although some
specimens have a very beautiful deep color.   Its
value is small.

Opal is a beautiful gem composed of silica in an
amorphous state, mixed with water. It is the same
mineral as quartz, with the addition of six or seven per
cent. of water. There are many varieties : the "noble,"
or precious, the "fire" reddish, the common, the semi-
opal, the cacholony milk-white, the hydrophane, opal
jasper, and the wood opal or opalized wood, etc. This
gem never occurs in a crystallized form ; its lustre is
vitreous inclining to resinous ; its hardness from 5.5 to
6.5 ; its specific gravity from 1.9 to 2.3, and is scratched
by quartz. It is soluble in a cold solution of caustic

potash. It is infusible before the blow-pipe, but gives off water and becomes opaque—those containing iron, red. The "noble" is a very brittle stone. Analysis gives the chemical composition of the different varieties as follows, viz. :

	Fire opal of Mexico. By Klaproth.	Fire opal of Georgia. By Bruch.	Precious opal of Hungary. By Damour.	Semi-opal of Hanau. By Stucker	Fire opal of Faroe. By Forcammerh
Silica.	92.00	91.89	93.90	82.75	88.73
Water	7.75	5.84	6.10	10.00	7.97
Peroxide of iron	0.25	. . . .	. . . .	3.00	. . . .
Alumina	. . . .	1.40	. . . .	3.50	0.49
Magnesia	. . . .	0.92	. . . .	. . . .	1.48
Lime	. . . .	. . . .	. . . .	0.25	0.49
Potash and soda	. . . .	. . . .	. . . .	. . . .	0.34

Precious opal is considered one of the most beautiful gems known. Held between the eye and light it appears of a pale or milky reddish blue, but seen by reflected light it displays all the colors of the rainbow in flakes, blotches or specks, and all the colors of the most beautiful gems are here seen in one. This wonderful play of colors is thought to arise from nearly invisible fissures, but Abbé Hatty ascribes it to thin films of air cavities in the interior. Opals are cut en cabochon on both sides, and its true beauties are only seen when the stone is moved about, when it seems to have actual life within itself. It is still more brilliant on a warm day. Fine specimens of a large size are rarely found. Mexican opal loses its beauty when exposed to water, but can be restored to its original color by a moderate application of heat. Sir Walter Scott alluded to this fact in "Anne of Geierstein," although he there ascribed

it to supernatural agency. After the publication of that
fiction the gem is said to have gone quickly out of fashion
in England, the belief that it was unlucky becoming so
prevalent; but they are again universal favorites, and
they are the only precious stones which defy imitation.
Common opal is used for cheap jewelry, cane tops, etc.
The other kinds are not used. Opal was known to the
most ancient authors, and was esteemed above every
other precious stone. Pliny says it unites the colors of
the ruby, topaz, amethyst and emerald in the most marvellous mixture, and that its fire is like the flame of
burning sulphur. He also relates that a Roman senator, Nonnius, was outlawed and exiled by Marcus
Antonius because he refused to give up an opal valued
at 20,000 sesterces, of the size of a filbert, and set in a
ring, and that the senator, rather than part with it, submitted to exile, carrying the stone with him. There
are two among the French crown jewels of wonderful
beauty. The finest known is in the museum at
Vienna, of great size and extraordinary beauty.
It is said a sum equal to $250,000 has been refused
for it.

The turqoise, formerly called Turkis or Turkey stone,
varies in color from white to a fine azure blue, sometimes greenish. The fine blue is the only kind of any
value; it is obtained in reinform or stalactitic masses,
never in crystals. It varies in hardness, and is numbered 6 in Moh's scale; it has a waxy lustre, occasionally translucent, generally opaque; its specific gravity
is 2.6; fracture conchoidal, with a white streak. Composition :

	Turquoise from Persia. By Herman.	Turquoise from Silesia. By Fohn.
Alumina	47.45	44.50
Phosphoric acid	27.34	30.90
Water	18.18	19.00
Protoxide of copper	2.02	3.75
Protoxide of iron	....	1.80
Peroxide of iron	1.10	....
Peroxide of manganese	0.50	....
Phosphate of lime	3.41	....

It decrepitates violently before the blow-pipe, and yields water. It is infusible, except with borax or salt of phosphorus. It dissolves in muriatic acid without effervescence; in the reducing flame it becomes brown, and gives the flame a green color. The stone found in Arabia Petræa, although of a dark, fine blue, changes its hue in a most mysterious and rapid manner, sometimes to a sickly green or whitish tint, or breaking out with white specks, or perhaps begins to whiten, or become green first round the edge; and therefore turquoises from that mine are not of so high value.

The Persian stone is also subject to change of color, but nothing like the proportion of the other, and ancient cameos and intaglios are extant which have retained their color to this day. Many persons still believe that this gem, by its changes, indicates the health of the wearer. The fact that it does vary its color in the most unaccountable manner may have something to do with this old superstition. The stone is cut en cabochon, and the Persian turquoise is much used in jewelry, also in oriental countries for ornamenting harness, girdles, pipes, daggers, swords, also for amulets and charms, often engraved with the Allah, a verse of the Koran, or some other device, and filled in with gold. The Shah of Persia is supposed to have all the finest specimens, allowing those of an inferior quality only to leave the country. This gem was known to the ancients by the name callaite, and believed to bring health and fortune to the wearer. Old specimens are to be seen in the Vatican, some of which have retained their color; they are likewise frequently met with in the ruins of ancient cities in Egypt, in the form of amulets.

Pearls are of almost every conceivable color and often of the most fantastic shapes, sometimes of considerable size and fine quality; but such are very rare. They are composed of carbonate of lime and organic matter. Its lustre is peculiar to itself, called pearly. Its specific gravity is 2.5 to 2.7. It is affected by acids and fetid gases, and calcines on exposure to heat. Panama pearls are heavier than the oriental. The sea pearl oyster (meleagrina margaritifera) is large, with a shell seven or eight inches in diameter, very thick, flat, and of a greenish-black exterior, with the interior of a silver white hue, reflecting various colors. This shell is the "mother of pearl" of commerce. The formation of the real pearl gem is accounted for by naturalists, with the supposition that the animal in trying to rid itself of some foreign body which has intruded into its shell, covers it with a deposit similar to the interior of that shell. Others ascribe it to a disease of the oyster. The Chinese, from a remote period, have been accustomed to insert small beads, images, etc., into the shells of oysters and mussels, and these have surely become coated with a pearly substance, but generally of a blackish tint, with little lustre, and very inferior to those formed by nature. The fine polish and lustre of pearls, which constitute its value, have never yet been even passably imitated. It would seem to be caused by the friction of the soft body of the oyster. The polish, in most cases, only exists on the outer surface or skin, on removing which it is dull in color and dead in lustre. Sometimes, however, pearls of bad exterior contain a fine and lively kernel. Some shells contain several pearls detached, some one or more adhering to the shell, and sometimes with pearls conglomerated together in a shapeless mass. Experiments have been made with a view of ascertaining the length of time required to produce large pearls, and the results would lead to the conclusion that the space of many years is necessary to develope them. This gem, from the most remote ages to the present, has been considered one of the richest gifts of nature. In the Bible it is mentioned, Job, ch. xxviii., and in Proverbs. Hindoo mythology ascribes to the god Vishnu the discovery or creation of pearls. The Persians, Babylonians, Egyptians, and other ancient nations held it in great esteem, and from them the Romans became acquainted with it; and the demend for them in ancient Rome was so great that they were sold there for fabulous prices. Seneca exclaims against the shameful extravagance of the Roman ladies in this particular. Pliny placed this gem next to the diamond in value, and supposed it to proceed from drops of dew swallowed by the oyster. In China pearls are used as medicine. In Bengal, at one time, virgins wore them

on their arms as a preserver of virtue. One of the
finest now known is called "La Peregrina," and is said
to be owned by a Russian princess. The Shah of
Persia has one valued at a sum equal to $300,000, and
the Imaum of Muscat one for which he refused $150,-
000. A pearl of the late Empress of the French was
one of the finest known. The beauty and value of
pearls depend on their form, color, texture, transparency, and lustre. The gem deteriorates by age, contact
with acids, gas, and noxious vapors, and should be
carefully kept.

There are other substances used in jewelry and for
personal adornment, such as coral, jet, lapis-lazuli, moon-
stone, amber, malachite, jade or nephite, etc., although
not belonging to the family of gems; and a short description of them will be given.

Amber varies in color, from white and pale yellow
to a deep brownish orange. It is very brittle, and yields
to the knife. It is a fossilized gum or resin, without
cleavage; hardness, 2 to 2.5, and specific gravity 1.081;
lustre resinous or waxy, and varies from transparent to
opaque. It burns readily, and gives an agreeable odor,
at 287°. It fuses and is decomposed, yielding water,
an empyreumatic oil, and succinic acid. It acquires
negative electricity by friction. It is composed of

    Carbon 80.99
    Hydrogen....................... 7.31
    Oxygen......................... 6.73
    Calcium 1.54
    Alumina........................ 1.10
    Silica. 0 63

Sir David Brewster, Goepert, and others, from experiments, have proved it to be of vegetable origin, as was
surmised by Pliny.   Yellow amber beads used to be in
fashion.   It is much used for the mouth-pieces of
pipes.

In oriental countries pipes, being lighted by a servant, amber was thought incapable of transmitting in-
fection.   It is also employed in chemistry, the oil of
amber and succinic being obtained from it by distilla-
tion, the residue serving for the manufacture of black
varnish.   The most valuable is nearly opaque, and
resembling fresh butter in color.   Amber was well
known to the ancients, and is frequently mentioned in
the classics.

Coral is not so much sought after as formerly, except
in China, India, and Persia, where it is ranked as one
of the most precious productions of nature, and immense
quantities are sent to those countries yearly.   It is cut
principally into beads, buttons, drops for ear-rings; also
leaves, flowers, and various other shapes; in charms,
worn in bunches, to avert the influence of the evil-eye.
The beads are used by the Brahmins and Fakirs for
rosaries, and the dead are adorned with coral ornaments
to prevent evil spirits from taking possession of the
corpse.   The deep red color, which harmonizes with
the olive skin of the Indian, is preferred, and but few
of the richer class of Indian girls are without one or two
coral ornaments.   It is also worn in Spain.   The Greeks
had a tradition that the blood dropping from the head of
Medusa, which Perseus had hung on some branches near

the sea-shore, becoming hard, was taken by sea nymphs and planted in the sea—hence coral.

By the Romans it was dedicated to Jupiter and Apollo. In the Middle Ages it was used in medicine as an astringent, and given to newly-born infants. When worn by men it was supposed to deepen in color, and to become paler when worn by women. Dioscarides, and also Boetius, sagely report it as efficacious against the delusions of the devil, when worn in the form of an amulet.

Jet is a variety of coal much used for mourning jewelry. It is blacker, tougher, and harder than ordinary coal, and when polished has considerable lustre. Its hardness is 1.5; specific gravity, 1.3; fracture, conchoidal. Great quantities of jet are sold in Spain and Turkey. Boetius says of this stone, that it secures men from nocturnal fears, spectres, and ghosts. Cordamus relates that the saints wore bracelets and rosaries of jet to number their prayers.

Jade or nephite, mostly used in Asia as jewelry is a hard, compact, translucent, tough stone, breaking with a splintery fracture and glistening surface. Its color varies from a creamy white to a dark green; hardness, 6 to 7; specific gravity, 2.9 to 3.1; slightly unctuous to the touch, and fuses with difficulty. It is not a distinct mineral, and its composition is variable. Two analyses are given:

	By Kattner.	By Schafhäutl.
Silica........................	50.50	58.90
Magnesia	31.00	22.42
Lime	....	12.28
Alumina.....................	10.00	1.32
Peroxide of Iron..............	5.50	2.70
Oxide of Chrome....	0.05	....
Water.......................	2.75	0.25
Peroxide of Manganese........	....	0.91
Potash......................	....	0.80

In Eastern countries it is carved into daggers and sword handles, cups, vases, etc.. and often inlaid with precious stones, the most favorite color being pale greenish-gray.   Good specimens bring a large price.

Moon-stone, once in fashion, is now seldom seen.   It is a kind of felspar or arthoclase, with a chatogant reflection, resembling that of cat's-eye, and of a pearly white color.   Its hardness, 6; specific gravity, 2.4 to 2.6; lustre, vitreous, inclining to pearly.   Composition,

Silica.........................64.00

Alumina.......................19.43

Lime 0.42

Water 1.14

Magnesia 0.20

Potash 14.31

It is cut en cabochon and is of but trifling value. The ancients prized it, employing it in their works of art.

Lapis-lazuli, a beautifully colored stone, has been sued from the earliest times for ornamental purposes;

it is of a rich blue color; opaque, with a subvitreous lustre; its hardness is 5.5; specific gravity, 2.38 to 2.45; it is found in masses, has an imperfect dodecahedral cleavage. It is seldom found in crystals, and when it is the specimens are small and of the rhombic dodeca-hedral form. Its composition is as follows:

Silica 46.0
Sulphuric acid.................... 4.0
Alumina........ .. ..14.5
Peroxide of iron.................. 3.0
Lime.............................17.6
Water 2.0
Carbonic acid....................10.0

It fuses to white glass; with borax it effervesces and becomes colorless; if calcined it loses its color, and gelatinizes in muriatic acid. It often has iron pyrites disseminated through it, which gives it the gold spotted appearance it often exhibits. The deep colored pieces are most esteemed, being used for studs and brooches as well as for vases, ornamental furniture, mosaic work, etc. Ground to powder they form the valuable pigment called ultramarine. I believe, however, an artificial substitute, costing much less, has been discovered near-ly as good as the genuine ultramarine.

Lapis-lazuli was well known to the ancients, and was the sapphire of the Greeks and Romans. Many fine specimens exist in old Italian and Spanish churches in slabs, pillars and other adornments to the altars and shrines; also, as panels on which are paintings. In the Russian palace of Zarskoeselo, is a room made by order of Catharine II., the walls of which are wholly covered with slabs of lapis and amber. The ancients used it in medicine as a purge.

Labrador felspar, Labradorite, is well known but not much used in jewelry; it possesses a brilliant multicolor of light-flashes similar to the opal. Its crystallization is of the triclinic system and is massive; specific gravity 2.67; hardness 6; lustre vitreous; easily cleavable; usually greyish, sometimes nearly white. Its composition is:

    Silica 55.75
    Alumina.........................26.50
    Peroxide of Iron................. 1.25
    Lime............................11.00
    Water........................... 0.50
    Soda........................... 4.00

It fuses to a colorless glass. Pulverized, it dissolves with heated muriatic acid; it is from translucent to semi-opaque; it will take a fine polish, and some specimens are very beautiful, owing to their chatoyant reflection.

Malachite, a beautiful copper ore, is a hydrous-carbonate of copper. Its hardness is 3.5; specific gravity 3.7; lustre vitreous, sometimes nearly adamantine; occasionally silky, often dull; color green-spotted and banded with other shades; it takes a high polish. Its composition, according to Klaprath:

    Carbonic acid.....................18.00
    Protoxide of Copper...............70.50
    Water.............................11.50

It is in great demand for ornamental purposes, but out of the large quantity annually found, only a small portion is adapted to this use—the compact variety, susceptible of a high polish, being very rare. It yields a large amount of metal, and is extensively used for smelting. In acids and ammonia it dissolves with effervescence.

CHAPTER XIII

THE Koh-I-Noor has had its history often told and with some variation. The Hindoo accounts deduce it from the time of the god Krisehna. It is known to have been in the treasury of Delhi, and taken at the conquest of that city by Ala-ed-Din. Thence it came into the possession of the Sultan Baber, of the Mogul dynasty in 1526. He esteemed it at the sum of the daily maintenance of the whole world. This gem was also seen by Tavernier among the jewels of Aurengzebe; it had then, however, been reduced from 793 carats to 186, by the unskillfulness of Hortensio Borgio, in an attempt to cut it; at which the Emperor Aurengzebe was so incensed, that he refused to pay Borgio the sum agreed on for the cutting, confiscated the whole of his possessions, and with great difficulty was persuaded to spare his life. Nadir Shah, the conqueror of India, obtained this stone by means of an artful trick, and from his descendants it passed into the hands of Acnmed Shah, whose son, Shah Sujah, was in turn forced to deliver it into the custody of Runjeet Singh. Soon after the capture of Lahore, at the time of the Sikh mutiny, it fell into the possession of the British troops, who presented it to Queen Victoria, June 3d, 1850, when it weighed 186 carats. It was exhibited in 1851, at the Crystal Palace, England. It was shown to several scientific men, among whom was Sir David Brewster; they were of opinion the stone presented great difficulties in the way of cutting. After much consideration, it was entrusted to Messrs. Gerrard, of the Haymarket, London, who gave it into the hands of Mr. Coster, of Amsterdam, who expressed himself confident of the result of recutting, and his work proved the correctness of his judgment. Although of less weight, it is of nearly the same size, and instead of a lusterless mass, like rock-crystal, it has become a brilliant, matchless for purity and fire. It now weighs 106⅟₆ carats, and forms one of the crown jewels of England.

The Braganza was found in 1741, in Brazil; it weighs 1,880 carats. But great doubt exists of its being a diamond; it belongs to the Portuguese crown jewels, and the government will not suffer it to be examined, and the facts cannot be ascertained regarding it. Many persons imagine it to be a white topaz.

The Mattam diamond belongs to the Rajah of Mattam, in Borneo; it was found about the year 1760, at Landak, Borneo, and has been the cause of a sanguinary war; it, nevertheless, remains in the possession of the Rajah. It is of pure water, weighs 367 carats, and is pear-shaped, indented at the thick end. The Dutch Governor of Batavia offered two gun-boats with stores and ammunition complete, and a sum equal to $250,000, for it; but the offer was refused—the Rajah replying, that on its possession depended the fortunes of his family.

The Cumberland diamond was presented to the Duke of Cumberland after the battle of Culloden, by the city of London, at a cost of £10,000. It was one of the stones claimed by the crown of Hanover, and has since been restored by the Queen of England. It weighs 32 carats, having been cut.

The Polar Star is a diamond remarkable for purity and brilliancy. In 1845 it was sold by a Russian Count, in London; afterwards it was purchased by a Russian Princess, in whose possession it now remains. Its weight is 40¼ carats.

The Eugénie Brilliant is an oval-shaped, perfect brilliant, of fifty-one carats, blunt at one end and very beautifully cut. It was purchased some years ago by the late Emperor, Napoleon III., for the Empress Eugénie.

The Sancy Diamond was found on the body of the Duke of Burgundy, after his death, and was afterwards, in 1479, bought by the king of Portugal, who sold it in 1489, to Nicolas de Barley, Baron de Sancy, after whom it is named. Sancy sent it to the king as a present, by the hand of a servant, who, being attacked by robbers, swallowed the stone, and after his death it was found in his body. Afterwards it was in the possession of James II. of England, who sold it to Louis XIV. of France, for the sum of £25,000. In the French Revolution, it disappeared along with a renowned blue diamond, which, strange to say, has never re-appeared. Subsequently the Sancy was sold by Goday, the Prince of Peace, who ruled Spain under Charles XIV. and Ferdinand VII., to Prince Paul Demidoff, who not long since parted with it to Sir Jamsetjee Jejeebhoy, for a sum equal to $100,000. It is an almond-shaped stone, weighing fifty-three and a half carats.

The Orloff Diamond is supposed to have formed one of the eyes of an idol in a Brahmin temple. It is said also to have been set in the famous peacock throne of Nadir Shah. Whatever its early history may have been, it was stolen by a Frenchman, who is reported to have been a priest at the shrine of some Brahmin god, and who sold it in Malabar for a sum equal to $14,000. It was purchased by the Armenian Schaffras, and subsequently, in 1774, sold to Catharine II., Empress of Russia, for 450,000 roubles, a pension of 20,000 roubles and a patent of nobility. It is now set in the sceptre of the Czar. It weighs 194¼ carats, is rose-cut, and has the under side flat like the Koh-I-Noor.

The Florentine Brilliant is supposed to have been one of the diamonds lost by Charles the Bold, Duke of Burgundy, at the battle of Granson. It was found by a Swiss soldier, who sold it to a priest for one florin; after which it was sold by a Genoese merchant to Ludovic Sforza, Duke of Milan; subsequently it came into possession of Pope Julius II., who gave it to the then Emperor of Austria, and it now belongs to the same monarchy. It weighs 139½ carats, is of a yellowish color, rather thick, covered with facets like a rose diamond, and pointed at both top and bottom.

The Regent or Pitt Diamond was purchased by Pitt, the Governor of Fort St. George, in Golconda, of Jamelchund, a Hindoo merchant, as he informs us in a pamphlet published to clear himself of the reports made of his having stolen it. Pope says:

> "Asleep and naked as the Indian lay,
> An honest factor stole the gem away."

Pitt sold it in the year 1717 to the Duke of Orleans, then Regent of France, for the large sum of £135,000. It was stolen from the Guard Mobile in 1792, but was restored in a mysterious manner. The Emperor Napoleon I. wore it in the pommel of his sword. It was shown at the French Exhibition of 1855, and formed a part of the French crown jewels. When rough, this stone weighed 410 carats, and its cutting cost a sum equal to $17,500, and occupied the space of two years. It now weighs 136¾ carats.

The Shah Diamond was presented by Cosroes, the son of Abbas Mirza, to the Emperor of the Russias; it is free from blemish, and perfectly pure, weighing 86 carats. It has a Persian inscription engraved on it, and a groove cut in the edge.

The Star of the South was found in 1853, at Bogagem, in Brazil, by a negro; when rough, it weighed 254⅛ carats; after being cut, 125 carats. It was cut by, and is the property of, Mr. Coster, of Amsterdam. It is oval-shaped, with considerable fire, and although not perfectly white and pure, is one of the finest large diamonds extant.

The Piggat, a diamond of 82½ carats, was sold in the last century by lottery, for about $150,000; afterwards it was bought by an English dealer for £6,000. It was then sold to the Pasha of Egypt for £30,000.

The Pasha of Egypt is a name given to a brilliant which belongs to Ibrahim Pasha. It weighs forty carats, is of octagonal form, brilliant cut, lively play and of very good quality.

The Nassak or Nassac Diamond was taken by the

Marquis of Hastings at the conquest of the Deccan, and was sold by the East India Company, in 1818, to Rundell and Bridge, an English house. When that firm retired from business, it was again sold, and by auction, becoming the property of the Marquis of Westminster. It now weighs 78¾ carats; before re-cutting it weighed 89¾ carats; it is of triangular shape with rounded facets.

The Hope Diamond, formerly owned by a Mr. Hope, is of a most brilliant sapphire, blue color; is unique of the kind; of oval form, well cut and proportioned. Since the disappearance of the French blue diamond, it is the most beautiful and important blue diamond in existence. It weighs 44½ carats, and at the International Exhibition at the Crystal Palace in 1851, it was universally admired.

Besides the above specified large diamonds, there are many others amongst the treasuries of the various countries. In the Russian treasury, a brilliant red of ten carats, for which Paul I. paid 100,000 roubles; in Portugal, one of 138½ carats, found in the river Abaite, Brazil, by three convicts. The Brazilian government, also, has some very large and curious stones. The Grand Duke of Tuscany is said to have one of a most beautiful blue, faceted all over. The Sultan of Turkey has two, one of 84 and one of 147 carats in weight. One of 76½ carats was lately owned by a city merchant of London, which was considered one of the finest in existence; drop shaped; its quality being superior to the Koh-I-Noor; it was found in Brazil. In the interior of India, Pegu, and China, there are said to be some

very large diamonds, but there are no authentic accounts
of them. The mines of South Africa will, without
doubt, bring into market many more quite large stones,
several of over a hundred carats' weight having already
been found there.

The value of gems and precious stones is so variable
that it is very difficult to fix a list of prices that would
be reliable for any period of time; and as this work is
not intended to be a guide to the trade, even at the
present time, it is not considered expedient to give any
list of prices. Jewels fluctuate in value like any other
article of commerce, and for large stones of rare beauty, no established price can ever be given, as it is
always a matter of negotiation, independent of any
market rates, and depending much on the necessity of
the seller and the desire of the buyer. When a diamond has a very decided color, such as blue, red, green,
etc., it is called a fancy stone and will bring a most
exhorbitant price.

In the celebrated work of Jeffries, the value of diamonds are based on the assumption that they increase
in value in proportion as the ratio of the square of its
weight. That is, supposing the value of a one
carat stone to be $20, a two carat will be worth
2 x 2=4 x 20=$80; one of three carats 3 x 3=9 x 20
=$180, etc., and he continues this mode of calculation
up to stones of one hundred carats, which would be
worth, by such calculation, 100 x 100=10,000 x 20
=$200,000. But at the present time it is hardly con-
sidered a correct rule, especially as applied to large
stones; still it was the rule of estimation at the South

African mines, to a great degree, but a rule applied to no other gems but the diamond.

The term first water, second water, etc., mean first quality, second quality, etc. A diamond, when perfect, should be clear as a drop of the purest water, the others are described as the second or third water, when more or less clear.

Many and great fluctuations in the price of diamonds have taken place since the discovery of the art of cutting: the value of money at times is also so much greater in proportion to the prices of the staples of life, that even if values were fixed and known, it could hardly be a guide to the retail merchant or purchaser.

In 1606, at a sale by auction at Venice, of the effects of Giovanni Ricardo, a great diamond merchant, as recorded by Partaleone, in his work called "Shilti Hogeborim," the value of a diamond of one carat was £21, 13s. 4d. In 1750, just before the discovery of the Brazilian mines, the price of a stone of the same weight was £8, and in 1791 only £6 was the value of a one carat stone. It is usually calculated that diamonds lose one-half their weight in cutting and polishing. From the details given under the head of each stone, the identity of any particular one can be readily determined. The jargoon and white sapphire are frequently confounded with the diamond; the pink topaz with the balas ruby; the jacinth with the cinnamon-stone, and the tourmaline with the emerald, not only by amateurs, but even by persons supposed to be acquainted with the properties of precious stones. With a little attention to the facts noted of each, it will prevent the possi-

11 *

bility of such error or fraud, and it is believed the more
the public are enabled to test by their senses, or such
simple means as may be easily available, the genuineness of gems, the more will their appreciation of jewels
increase.

APPENDIX.

WORKS ON THE SUBJECT OF GEMS.

For the benefit of persons who desire to pursue this subject further, a partial list of the many works on precious stones is annexed. Besides the following there are almost hundreds of books on the same subject, published at different times in France, Germany and other European countries, in their respective languages, and many in the Latin language, some of which have already been cited.

Probably there is as much literature on the subject of precious gems as upon any subject connected with natural science or natural history, even from the first writers of ancient times to the present day

ANDRADA (M. D.) An Account of the Diamonds of Brazil. Nich. Journ., i., 24. 1797.

BARLINGTON (Charles). A Systematic Arrangement of Minerals, their Chemical, Physical, and External Characters. 4to. London.

BOUILLON (De la Grange). Analysis of the Substance Known by the Name of Turquoise. Nich. Journ., xxi., 182.

BOURNON (Count de). An Analytical Description of the Crystalline Forms of Corundum from the East Indies and China. Phil. Trans., abr. xviii., 368. 1798.

Also by the same. A Description of the Corundum Stone, and its Varieties, commonly known as Oriental Ruby, Sapphire, etc. Phil. Trans., p. 223. 1801.

By the same author. A Descriptive Catalogue of Diamonds in the Cabinet of Sir Abraham Hume. 4to. London. 1815.

BOYLE (Hon. Robert). An Essay about the Origin and Virtues of Gems, with some Conjectures about the Consistence of the Matter of Precious Stones, etc. London. 8vo. 1672. And 12mo. 1673.

By the same. Experiments and Considerations upon Color, with Considerations on a Diamond that Shines in the Dark. 8vo. London.

BREWSTER (Sir David, LL.D., F.R.S.L., etc.) On the Optical Properties of Muriate of Soda, Fluate of Lime, and the Diamond, as Exhibited in their Action upon Polarized Light. Phil. Trans., viii., 157. 1817.

BREWSTER (same). On a New Optical and Mineralogical Property of Calcareous Spar. 4to. Edingb. 1815.

BREWSTER (same). On the Effects of Compression and Dilatation Altering the Polarizing Structure of Doubly-refracting Crystals. 4to. Edingb. 1818.

BREWSTER (same). On the Optical Properties of Sulphuret of Carbon, etc., with Inferences respecting the Structure of Doubly-refracting Crystals. Fol. Edingb. 1819.

CHEVENIX (Richard, Esq., F.R.S.). Analysis of Corundum and some Substances that Accompany it. Phil. Trans., p. 327. 1802.

DAVY (Sir Humphrey, Prof. of Chem., etc., etc.) Some Experiments on Combustion of the Diamond and other Carbonaceous Substances. Phil. Trans., p. 557. 1814.

DAVY (same). Description of the Diamond. Phil. Trans., abr. ii., 405. 1708.

DAVY (same). The Diamond, or the Pest of a Day. Fores 4to. London. 1797.

DINGLEY, (Robert, Esq.) On Gems and Precious Stones, Particularly such as the Ancients Used to En-grave on. Phil. Trans., abr. ix, 395. 1797.

EMANUEL (Harry, F. R. G. S.) Diamonds and Pre-cious Stones. London. 1867.

ELLIOT (John, F. R. S.) On theSpecific Gravity of Diamonds. Phil. Trans., abr. ix, 147. 1745.

FRUCHTVANGER (Dr. L). A Popular Treatise on Gems, in Reference to their Scientific Value, etc. 8vo. New York. 1859.

Genuine Account of the State of the Diamond Trade in the Dominion of Portugal; with some Authentic Pieces, in a Letter from a Merchant in Lisbon, to his Correspondent in London. 4to. London. 1785.

GREGOR (Rev. William M. A.) Analysis of a Va-riety of the Corundum. Nich. Journ., iv, 209. 1803.

GUYTON MOREAU (B. L.) Account of Certain Experiments and Inferences Respecting the Combustion of the Diamond, and the Nature of its Composition. Nich. Journ., iii, 298.

GUYTON (the same.) On the Singular Crystallization of the Diamond. Nich. Journ., xxv, 67. 1810.

GUYTON (the same.) Verbal Process of the Conversion of Soft Iron into Cast Steel, by Means of the Diamond. Nich., Journ., iii, 353. 1799.

Hertz (B.) Catalogue of Mr. Hope's Collection of Pearls and Precious Stones, Systematically Arranged and Described. 4to. London. 1839.

HINDMARSH (R.) Precious Stones. Being an Account of the Stones Mentioned in the Sacred Scriptures. 8vo. London. 1851.

History of Jewels. 12mo. London. 1671.

HODGSON (Rev. John.) Dissertation on an Ancient Cornelian. Archæol. ii, 42. 1773.

JEFFRIES (David, Jeweler). Treatise on Diamonds and Pearls, in which their Importance is Considered, Plain Rules are Exhibited for Ascertaining their Value, and the True Method of Manufacturing Diamonds is laid down. 8vo. 30 copper plates. London. 1750–51–53.

JEFFRIES (the same). An Abstract of the Treatise on Diamonds and Pearls, by which the Usefulness to all who are any way Interested in these Jewels will Sufficiently Appear. 8vo. London. 1759.

KLAPROTH (Martin Henry).   Analysis of the Spinel.
Nich. Journ., iii, 588.   1799.

LABARTE (M. Jules).   Hand-Book of the Arts of the
Middle Ages, and Renaissance as Applied to the Decora-
tion of Jewels, Arms, etc.   8vo.   London. 1855.

LEONARDUS (Camillus).   The Mirror of Stones in
which the Nature, Generative Properties, Virtues, and
Various Species of more than 200 Different Jewels,
Precious and Rare Stones are Distinctly Described.
8vo.   London.   1750.

MACCULLOCK (John, M. D., F. L. S.)   Remarks on
Several Parts of Scotland which Exhibit Quartz Rocks,
and on the Nature and Connection of this Rock in
General.   Geol. Trans., i, 650.   1811.

MACKENZIE (Sir George Stewart, Bart., F. R. S. L. &
E.)   Experiments on the Combustion of the Diamond,
the Formation of Steel by its Combination with Iron,
etc.   Nich. Journ., iv, 103.   1800.

MACKENZIE (the same).   On the Formation of Chalcedony.   4to.   Phil. Trans.   London.

HOWE (John).   A Treatise on Diamonds and Precious Stones, Including their History, Natural and
Commercial, and the Best Method of Cutting and Polishing them.   8vo.   London.   1813.

MORTIMER (Cromwell, M. D.)   Remarks on the Precious Stone Called Turquoise.   Phil. Trans., abr. viii.,
324.   London.

Notter (Laurentius). A Treatise on the Ancient Method of Engraving Precious Stones Compared with the Modern. Fol. London. 1754.

Nichols (Thomas). Gemmarius Fidelis : or the Faithful Lapidary, Experimentally Describing the Richest Treasures of Nature, in an Historical Narrative of the Several Natures, Virtues, and Qualities of all Precious Stones, with a Discovery of all such as are Adulterate and Counterfeit. 4to. London. 1659.

Nichols (the same). Arcula Gemmæ ; or, the Nature, Virtue, and Value of Precious Stones, with Cautions for those who Deal in them. 4to. Cambridge. 1750.

Nichols (the same). A Lapidary ; or, History of Precious Stones, with Cautions for the Undeceiving of all those that Deal with them. 4to. Cambridge, Eng. 1752.

Portsch (P). Catalogue of the Geological Cabinet of Vienna, with a Bibliographical List of Works Treating on the Subjects of Geology, Oryctology, and Paleontology. 8vo. Vienna. 1864.

Pepys (William Hasledine, Treasurer of the Geol. Soc.) On the Quantity of Carbon in Carbonic Acid, and on the Nature of Diamond. Phil. Trans., p. 267. 1807 ; and Nich. Jour., xix, 267.

Pliny. Historia Naturalis. Var. Ed.

Pole (W.) Diamonds. 8vo. London Archaeol. Trans. London. 1861.

POETA (Giov. Baptista). A Method of Knowing the Inward Virtues of Things by Inspection. Fol. Neapoli. 1601.

SANDIUS (Christopher). On the Origin of Pearls. Phil. Trans., abr. ii., 126. 1674.

SARMENTO (James Castro de, M. D.) An Account of Diamonds found in Brazil. Phil. Trans., abr. vii., 503. 1731.

STRACHAN. Observations on Coral, Large Oysters. Rubies, etc. Phil. Trans., abr. iv., 711. 1701.

SWEDENSTIERNA (E. F.) An Account of the Swedish Corundum from Gellivara, in Lapland. Geol. Trans., iii., 415. 1816.

TAVERNIER. Travels in Turkey, Persia, and the Indies. 4to. Paris. 1676.

TENNANT (Smithson, Esq., F. R. S.) On the Nature of the Diamond. Phil. Trans., xviii., 97. 1797; and Nich. Jour., i., 177. 1797.

THEOPHRASTUS. History of Stones, with the Greek Text and the English Version and Notes, Critical and Philosophical, Including the Modern History of Gems Described by that Author. By Sir John Hill. 8vo. London. 1746.

VANQUELIN (Citizen). Information Respecting the Earth of the Beryl. Nich. Jour., ii., 393.

VANQUELIN (the same).   Analysis of the Crysolite of the Jewelers, Proving it to be Phosphate of Lime. Nich. Jour., ii., 414.

VANQUELIN (the same).   Analysis of the Aquamarine or Beryl, etc.   Nich. Jour., ii., 358.

VEGA (Garcilaso de la,).   History of the Incas. Var. Ed.

www.ingramcontent.com/pod-product-compliance
Lightning Source LLC
Chambersburg PA
CBHW030404270326
41926CB00009B/1259